RIGHTS OF WOMEN

IN DIFFERENT ASPECTS
UNDER THE LAW

SHRADDHA VERMA

TRUE SIGN
PUBLISHING HOUSE

Published by True Sign Publishing House
Address: SY. No. 21/2 & 21/3, Sonnenahalli,
Krishnarajapura, Bengaluru,
Karnataka - 560049 India
E-mail: truesignbooks@gmail.com
Website: www.truesign.in

**Rights Of Women
In Different Aspects Under The Law**

Author: Shraddha Verma

ISBN: 978-93-5904-993-9

First Edition: 2023

CONTENTS

Rights of Women in Different Aspects Under the Law

Introduction

Women do not need to be polite to someone who is making them feel uncomfortable. You know, what I mean right?

If this is being read by a female, I'm probably hitting my goal. In India, it is seen that women are not much aware of their rights and that continues to remain recessive in society. Only a person who is well aware can discern between just and unjust and this article would surely help you become just.

In India, there is no paucity of laws for women. Our Constitution provides exclusive rights to women for their protection and development. Furthermore, **IPC, CrPC** and **Evidence Act** are also active when it comes to women and their protection. We have some special laws as well for effective implementation of the rights of women against abuse, Harassment, violence, inequality, etc.

Rights Within Marriage

Matrimonial Rights of Women

Introduction

In India, upon marriage, women leave their parental homes and live in the home provided by the husband or by his family members. This home is called her matrimonial home. (In fact traditionally it is believed that after marriage a woman has rights only in her husband's home and not in her parental home, though legally the position is now changed and today women have a right of residence in both parental as well as the matrimonial home.)

The contract of marriage creates a legal obligation upon the husband and his family members to provide a shelter and maintenance to the wife. In our society, a woman is perceived as a home maker, in addition to all other roles she may be required to perform. So while women have the burden of managing the house, cooking for the family, raising the children and tending to the sick, their chances of earning an adequate income to support themselves or even the chances of retaining their pre-marriage jobs are constrained. Hence, when economic support is withdrawn due to a matrimonial conflict, most women are rendered destitute.

The situation becomes dismal when they have the additional burden of caring for their children. Women's right to shelter and maintenance is located within this conceptual framework. There are various legal provisions which are meant to safeguard the rights of the wife in her husband's home and to ensure that she can live there with dignity and safety. The husband and his family cannot deprive her of these rights. They cannot harass a wife for dowry and inflict violence upon her. If a situation of domestic or sexual violence arises, the wife can avail legal remedies under criminal as well as civil laws. The wife also has a right to file for divorce and opt out of the marriage. She also has the right of custody of her children.

a. Right to Live in the Matrimonial Home

What is a Matrimonial Home?

When a woman is married, she acquires the right to live in her husband's home. This home becomes the woman's matrimonial home. Even if it is not owned by her husband and is in the name of his parents or siblings, she still has a right to reside in this house and she cannot be thrown out of this house. A widow cannot be thrown out from the house in which she was living with her husband, after her husband's death. It does not matter if the house was not owned by her husband.

The term used in the Protection of Women from Domestic Violence Act (Domestic Violence Act or DV Act, for short) is — shared household.

A shared household is where the woman resides or has resided (i.e. has left or has been thrown out) with the man in a domestic relationship [S. 2(s) of the DV Act].

It does not matter that the shared household is not owned by either the woman or the man i.e. the house is on lease/license or joint family property. This right is protected under S. 17 of the Domestic Violence Act. If she is thrown out the court can pass an order to put her back in the home. The court can also ask the respondent to provide alternative accommodation if the woman does not want to return to a violent home.

How can women protect her right ?

In order to protect this right, a woman must first believe that by virtue of her marriage, she has acquired a right to reside in her husband's home and she cannot be dispossessed from this home. Most often, women lose their right to their matrimonial home because they themselves do not believe that they have a right to reside there. Even when they are asked to leave the home, they must believe that they have a right to reside in the home and this right can be protected by law. This is the first step.

Only when women believe this, the right can be protected by law. If there is an apprehension that she will be thrown out of this house, she must approach a magistrate's court under the provisions of the Domestic Violence Act and obtain an order of injunction to restrain her husband or his family members from dispossessing her (throwing her out) from her matrimonial home (Ss.17, 19 of DV Act). This will secure her right of residence in this house. In the event that the husband or his family members violate this order they will be liable for punishment under the Domestic Violence Act. (S.31 of DV Act).

A woman will be deprived of this right only when an alternate accommodation of a permanent nature is provided for her. Until such time, her right to reside in the matrimonial home will be protected by the court.

b. Right to Claim Maintenance for Self and Children

What is Maintenance?

The law imposes a legal obligation on the husband to provide maintenance to his wife. If he fails to provide for her, the wife can approach the court for an order of maintenance.

The term—maintenance is the amount required for a decent living, including cost of food, shelter (if the same is not provided by the husband), travel, requirements of health care, educational, extra-curricular and recreational expenses of children, and other sundry expenses.

Who can Claim Maintenance?

Under our law, the wife, minor children, major children who suffer from physical or mental disabilities, unmarried major daughters and aged parents are entitled to maintenance as they are unable to maintain themselves.

Can the wife claim maintenance for her children along with herself?

Yes, the wife can claim maintenance for herself and her children. If the children are living separately along with their mother, they also have an independent right to claim maintenance from their father. If a woman is working, can she still claim maintenance? Even if a woman is working, she can claim maintenance, if her husband's income is substantially more than her income and she is unable to maintain herself or her children from that income. If the husband and wife are earning the same amount, she cannot claim maintenance from him. But in such a situation, women can claim maintenance for their children.

Can a woman who is living with her husband claim maintenance?

Yes, if her husband is not providing her maintenance while she is living in the same house with him, she has a right to claim maintenance. Can women claim maintenance during divorce? Yes. If a woman files for divorce, in the same petition, she can also claim interim and permanent maintenance for herself and for her children. Along with this she also needs to make a separate application for interim maintenance which can be taken up at the initial stage and decided so she will start getting some maintenance while her petition for divorce is pending in the court. If her husband has filed for divorce, as soon as she received the papers, she can immediately file an application for interim maintenance which will be heard and decided first as a preliminary issue.

Is a woman entitled to claim maintenance after her divorce?

Yes. Even after divorce, if she has not received a lumpsum amount as alimony, which is adequate to meet her expenses, she can claim maintenance from her husband until she remarries.

If during litigation, the husband agrees to take the wife back will she still be entitled for maintenance?

Usually, in order to prevent an order of maintenance being passed against him, the husband may volunteer to take the wife back or may even file proceedings for—restitution of conjugal rights. If a woman is keen to reconcile with her husband, she may accept this offer, but if there is a history of violence, then she must exercise caution before accepting it, because once an order is passed dismissing the petition on the ground that the parties have reconciled, it will be difficult for the woman to start the proceedings all over again, as it would be deemed that she has condoned (or forgiven) the husband for his earlier acts of cruelty. Hence, it is advisable to stipulate certain conditions or even keep the proceedings pending in the court for a few months, to ensure that the husband is sincere in his offer of reconciliation and is not doing so only to avoid payment of maintenance, before the earlier petition is withdrawn.

What is the criterion to decide the amount of maintenance?

The amount of maintenance awarded should be sufficient to meet the regular household expenses, children's educational, medical, recreational expenses, to pay the rent of the dwelling house, etc. It should be sufficient to meet the basic needs of a person. Here the standard of life that a person is used to is also taken into consideration. For instance, if the husband is very rich and the wife is used to that lifestyle she will be given a higher amount than a person earning a modest income where the wife is used to a modest life. Hence, it is important to collect evidence to prove the husband's lifestyle and income such as type of house, area of the house, type of car or two wheeler, property details, trips to foreign countries, etc. The exact amount is decided as per the income of the husband and the needs of the wife and children.

Tips: Many a time, husbands try to show that their earnings are far less than their actual income by showing old salary slips or by hiding their additional income. So it is necessary for the wife to get all the information before approaching the court, and collect the necessary details – recent salary record, bank statements, income from business or from family property, income tax returns, etc.

Is it necessary to file for divorce while filing for maintenance?

No. If the woman does not wish to file for divorce, she can make an application only for maintenance. This can be done under the provisions of S.125 Cr.PC or under the Domestic Violence Act without filing for divorce.

Cases Related to Matrimonial Rights of Women

Rights of Mothers for Custody of Children

Introduction

Right of custody of their children is a very important concern for women facing domestic abuse. Due to the fear of losing custody of their children, many women continue to live in violent relationships and are afraid of taking legal recourse to end the violence. Earlier, the father was considered as the natural guardian - there is a belief prevalent in society that the children belong to the husband and his family and the woman has no claim over them and that her role is confined to only taking care of them. When women leave their matrimonial home, they are often warned that they will not be able to get custody of their children and further, they will not be even able to meet them. But over the years, due to sustained struggle from the women's movement, the law is changed and today the woman is considered as the joint natural guardian of her children and also considered as the primary caretaker of her children. The courts also consider that she will be the best suited person to take care of her children. In this section, women's right to custody and the ways in which this right can be secured is explained.

a. Situations where custody of children becomes contentious and precautions which women must take, What right do women, as mothers, have over their children?

A wife, along with her husband, has the right of custody and guardianship over her children. As the primary caretaker of her children, she is responsible for their care and protection. Hence, she is entitled to their custody and guardianship.

When does the issue of custody of children arise?

The issue of custody of children arises if due to a dispute between the spouses, if either of the parties or both, wish to live separately from each other. When she is separating from her husband, how can the woman retain the custody of her children? If she is separating from her husband, the best way to retain custody of the children is for the wife to take the children along with her when she is leaving her matrimonial home. If the children are already residing with the mother, usually interim custody will be retained with the mother, even if the husband approaches the court for custody of the children. It is important for any one advising the woman (e.g. lawyer, NGO member, counselor, etc.) to give women accurate advise regarding this, to avoid unwarranted anxiety about the issue of securing the legal custody of their children later during court proceedings.

Why don't women usually take the children along with them?

This is because women think that if they take their children with them, the husband may file a police complaint against them that they have kidnapped the children. However, the police have no right to do this as she is the mother and hence she is also the natural guardian of her children. A case of kidnapping cannot be filed against a natural guardian.

Is it possible for the woman to take custody of her child after she has left the home?

If a woman has not taken her children with her when she is leaving the house, it is possible to take the custody later. This can be done with the help of a member of a local Mahila Mandal/NGO, a social worker, or the local police, soon after she has left the home. If the child left behind is very young and cannot live without the love and care of the mother, or if the woman is breast feeding her child, this must be done at the earliest. If there is a long gap after the woman has left the home, it will not be possible to take custody in this manner, as the child may get used to living with the father and his family and may not wish to come with the mother. In such a situation it is advisable to approach the court for appropriate orders.

Caution: If the child is attached to the husband or his mother and does not wish to come with the mother, it will not be possible to take the custody of the child. Always remember that the child's wishes and well- being are the most important factors in matters of custody.

Can the husband file a police complaint against her for kidnapping the child?

No, if the child wants to be with the mother and the mother wishes to have the child with her, the husband cannot file a case of kidnapping against her as she is the natural guardian of the child. However, only the mother alone has a right to take custody of her child. No one else can do it on her behalf, but a support person or a social worker can help her or accompany her. At times the police may refuse to help the woman and may insist on a court order. The principle, the best interest of the child is paramount.

What is the main principle which the courts rely upon while deciding the matter of the custody of children?

The only principle which is applied while deciding the custody of children - the best interest of the child is important. (This principle enshrined in the **United Nations Declaration of the Rights of the Child** is relied upon by Indian Courts while determining the parental rights for custody of children.) This means the custody must be given to the person who is best suited to take care of the child or to the parent who is the primary caretaker of the child. In the Indian setting, usually this person is the mother.

What factors are considered by the court while deciding the "best interests of the child"?

The love and care given to the child is the most important factor. The general growth of the child, the child's well-being, progress in school, child's own preference, the atmosphere in the home - these are some of the factors which are considered while deciding the 'best interests of the child'. Generally, whoever has physical custody of the child at the point of approaching the court usually gets to retain the custody. However, this rule is not rigid and if the situation so demands, custody can be changed from one parent to the other, as per the court order. Usually, if the child is older, while changing the custody, the court will ascertain the views of the child.

Caution: If a woman is facing domestic violence and she is desirous of leaving her matrimonial home to escape from violence, she must be given correct advice that she has a right to take her children along with her, and that she does not require a court order to do this.

Is it true that the law considers the father as the "natural guardian" of the children and hence his right over the children is superior to that of the mother?

No this is not true. This was the belief earlier. Within the patriarchal family system, the father was considered as the head of the family' and the 'natural guardian' of the children. Both the wife and the children belonged to the husband; but gradually this belief changed. Now our law considers both father and mother as equal partners in marriage and also considers them as equal guardians of their children. The father's rights over the child are not superior to that of the mother. However, traditional values still prevail and many people still endorse this anti-women view and legally incorrect view.

Is it true that the mother's rights over the custody of a child under five years is superior to that of the father?

Yes, this is true. This is because a young child needs the love and care of the mother and hence the law considers that the mother is better equipped to look after a child of tender age. The child may also be breast fed by the mother. Depriving the child of the mother's love and care may cause great trauma and anxiety to the child. In such cases, if the mother is thrown out, the police can help the mother to get immediate custody of the child, to save the child from being subjected to such trauma. If the mother is employed, will she still be given custody of the child? This is a general misconception that prevails in society. People feel that if the woman is employed, she will not get custody of the child as she has no time to look after the child and the father's mother may be more suitable to look after the child. But this is not true. The right of the mother is superior to that of the husband's mother. A woman will not be deprived of the custody of the child just because she is working or has a demanding job.

If the father is very affluent and if the mother does not have sufficient means to bring up the child, will she lose custody of the child?

Even if the father is very affluent, a mother will not be deprived of the custody of her child only on this ground. It is usual in our society that the father has better financial resources in most cases, and the woman may have been a housewife all her life. She may not even have the requisite qualifications to earn an adequate income. But this factor alone cannot be taken into consideration while deciding the issue of custody of the child. The one who is able to provide the best love and care for the child will be the only deciding factor. At times people feel that if the mother is unemployed she may not get custody as she does not have the financial resources to bring up the child. However, since the legal obligation to provide for the child is primarily with the father, the fact that the mother does not have sufficient means to provide for the child will not be considered as a major obstacle while awarding her the custody of her child. So, the bottom line is that it does not matter if the woman is employed or unemployed.

If the husband accuses the wife of committing adultery, will she be entitled to claim custody of her children?

Accusing the wife of adultery or of loose moral character is the usual ploy adopted by the husband or his lawyer to deprive the wife of her right to custody of children because they are under a misconception that a woman who has committed adultery will not be entitled to custody of her children. But the factual position is that the issue of custody of child will be decided only on who is the main caretaker of the child, what kind of environment the mother is able to provide for the well-being of the child and not on whether she has committed any matrimonial fault. Since this ploy is used routinely by lawyers, courts do not give it serious consideration. However, many women get traumatized when they find that such baseless allegations are leveled against them. It is best to ignore these allegations and focus on the core issues regarding custody.

If the mother remarries after her divorce will she lose the custody of her child?

No, if she has been looking after the child well, she will not lose custody when she remarries. When the court decides on the matter of custody, the court will look only at the best interests of the child. The child's wishes will be taken into consideration. If the child is happy with the mother, the mother will not be deprived of the custody of her child upon her remarriage. Even the local (or caste) panchayat or the jamaat cannot force the mother to give up the custody of her child upon her remarriage. If this happens, she must not comply with the order, and instead immediately must file an application for custody under the Domestic Violence Act and protect her rights.

Rights of a non-custodial parent if custody of the child is given to one parent, what right does the non-custodial parent have?

It is important that the child has the love and care of both the parents. It is necessary for the healthy upbringing of a child. Hence, if one's parent is given custody, the other parent will be given the right of access. This means if the child is living with the mother, the child may meet the father on a regular basis i.e. once a week, on a Sunday or once a fortnight during the weekend, etc. Similarly during the holidays, the father will be given some days to spend with the child. Sometimes the holidays are divided equally between the parents. Usually the court issues strict guidelines regarding the timings for access, which both parties must strictly comply with.

What care should the parents take so that the child grows up in a healthy environment?

The parent who has custody of the child must look after the child's physical and emotional needs well so that the child's personality develops well. The educational needs of the child are also an important factor and the parent who has custody must ensure that all educational needs of the child are met according to the standard of life enjoyed by the parents.

Case Related to Custody of Child

Vishnu Ubale vs Mrs. Archana Tushar Ubale,

gave shape to the concept of shared custody by denying exclusive custody of an eight-year-old girl to any one parent. Instead, Justice PL Palsingankar, on consultation with parenting experts presented a detailed shared parenting plan for the child's upbringing. It eliminated the need for a primary guardian giving both parents equal rights over the custody of their child.

Muhammad Tahir vs. Raees Fatima,

the Supreme Court disallowed the father's petition for custody of the minor children and disagreed with his contention that he was allowed to take custody from the mother because the mother was illiterate, had no source of income and that she had developed an illicit relationship with another person. The consideration of welfare of the child in custodial matters is interpreted in such a way so as to merely provide lip service to the ideal. In reality, matters related to preconceived notions of gender stereotypes have an unnecessary importance.

Protection under the Domestic Violence Act

What is "domestic violence" under the Protection of Women from Domestic Violence Act?

The term—domestic violence under Domestic Violence Act includes physical, emotional, sexual and economic violence (S.3). The following is an explanation of these terms. Physical violence - beating, kicking, slapping, etc emotional violence – abusing, using derogative words, demanding dowry, humiliating her because she does not have children or has only girl children, or because she is not good looking or she has not brought enough dowry, etc or threatening to throw her out of the house or threatening that she will not be provided any money for her or her children's maintenance, etc.

Sexual violence forcing the wife to have sex when she is not in a position to have sex (e.g. during menstruation or soon after delivery/ abortion), forcing her to watch pornography, filming her nude and then circulating these video clips, threatening to bring other women into the house to have sex with them in her presence, forcing the wife to have sex with other men, etc. Economic abuse means neglecting to maintain the wife, not giving her money for her maintenance, throwing her out of the house and not providing any shelter or maintenance, not returning her dowry, stridhan or jewellery, etc.

The husband has to pay for the woman's regular household expenses and for the children's expenses. If he does not pay her regular maintenance or abandons the wife, it would amount to domestic violence under this Act.

What rights does this Act give women?

The Act gives women the right to live a life free from violence. It protects the right to shelter in the following ways :-

Right to an order of protection:

If there is a threat of violence, the woman can get an order of protection, restraining the husband and his family members from committing violence on her. Even if she is living in her own father's house and if she is afraid that the husband may assault her or come to her place of work and humiliate her, she can ask for a—stop order (injunction) to restrain him from coming anywhere near her (S.18).

Right to live in the same house:

The husband, father-in-law or even the father of a woman/girl cannot throw her out from the house where she is living or has lived (S.19).

Right to claim maintenance:

As explained above, the woman has a right to claim maintenance under this Act (S.20)

Right to custody:

No one can take away the children from the mother, not even the father. If such a threat is there, she can go to court and get an order to protect her right. If her child is taken away forcibly from her custody she can approach the police or the court to get her child back (S.21).

Right to claim compensation:

If the woman has suffered any harm or injury due to domestic violence she has a right to claim compensation for it under the Act (S.22).

Note: The woman has the right to take with her all her belongings i.e. clothes, jewellery, valuables, money, etc. This is her stridhan. She can take help to retrieve her belongings from a local NGO, the police or the court. The remedy is also available under S.19 (8) of the D.V.Act. If her husband or in-laws do not return her belongings (stridhan) at the time of leaving the home, she can also file a police complaint under section 406 of the IPC.

Against whom can the woman get the orders under this Act?

A woman can get orders under this Act against her husband, father-in-law, brother-in- law, etc. She can also get orders against the female relatives of the husband such as mother-in-law or sister-in-law, if they have contributed to causing domestic violence to the woman. Every woman can claim relief under this Act, irrespective of their religion, including Muslims as the Act stipulates that any woman can claim relief under this Act. The Act defines the aggrieved person in very broad terms as—Any woman/

child facing domestic violence from an adult male with whom she shares a domestic relationship and is living/has lived within a shared household [S.2(a)].

Who should a woman approach to file a complaint?

The woman can approach the Protection Officer, a private lawyer, a legal aid lawyer or a local NGO to help her in approaching the court to protect her rights. She can also go to a police station and the police will refer her to the Protection Officer in the area. If she is injured she can go to a hospital and the hospital will help her to reach the police or the Protection Officer of the area.

What advice should be given to the woman before she files her complaint?

The woman must be advised that when she is leaving the house where she has lived with her husband or in-laws, she must take with her, her belongings and valuables, her children, her documents such as her educational certificates, copy of other documents such as birth or marriage certificate, caste certificate, husband's bank pass book, or bank statement, contract of employment, etc.

Caution: The woman must collect evidence before leaving or filing the complaint to support her statements. This could include medical reports of injuries, earlier complaints to police, etc. Also documents such as house papers to prove ownership of house, ration card, 7/12 extract as proof of land ownership or income from the land, any other proof to show husband's income, etc are important to prove the husband's income.

Who is a 'Protection Officer' under the Act?

A 'Protection Officer' (PO) is a government officer designated or appointed by the Ministry of Women and Child Development, who is entrusted with the duty of providing all kinds of support to the woman including helping her to approach the court, taking her to a shelter home if she needs shelter, taking her to a hospital if she needs medical help or helping her to access other government schemes to help women. The total number of Protection Officers in Maharashtra are around 670. This number includes the officers who are designated as Protection Officers as well as those specially appointed as Protection Officers.

How to approach a court for an order?

Each time a woman is beaten and she approaches the Protection Officer, a **(Domestic Incident Report (DIR-Form I)** is prepared. This provides a proof of domestic violence. If the woman has gone directly to a private lawyer, then the lawyer will prepare a detailed application and also an application for interim reliefs. In such case there is no need to approach a Protection Officer and obtain a DIR. If she has any evidence then that can also be mentioned (for instance if earlier a police complaint was filed by her or if she has gone to the hospital when she was injured due to the beating, etc.) All proofs of husband's income can be attached if the woman is seeking an order of maintenance under the DV Act. In the end, it must be clearly stated as to what type of remedies she is seeking (e.g. protection, maintenance, residence, custody of child, etc.)

How long will it take to obtain an order?

This Act is supposed to provide quick reliefs. The court dates are given at short intervals. It is possible to get an interim order within a month of filing the proceedings. Though the final orders are supposed to be given within 60 days, due to technical difficulties and workload of the court, this does not usually happen. But the final order can be expected within one year of filing and an interim order can be expected at least within two months.

Violence Against Women and Children

Dowry Harassment and Cruelty Against Wives

What is the meaning of Dowry?

Section 2 of the Dowry Prohibition Act (DPA), 1961 defines—dowry as any cash, jewellery, valuables, or property which the husband or his family members demand from the bride's parents at the time of marriage, as a consideration of marriage. This term also includes demands made subsequent to the marriage from the bride or her parents.

Is demanding dowry an offence?

Yes, it is a serious offence under the Dowry Prohibition Act, 1961. It is punishable with a minimum of five years' imprisonment and a fine of Rs.15, 000/- or equal to the value of the dowry demanded or paid.

Who can register a complaint under this Act?

The woman herself, her parents, the police, Dowry Prohibition Officer appointed under S.8-B of the Act, or even a non-governmental organization on behalf of the woman, can register a complaint.

Which are the provisions related to Dowry Related Violence in the Indian Penal Code (IPC)?

After the anti-dowry violence in early 1980 several women's organizations demanded stringent punishment for husbands and their family members if they caused any dowry related violence to a newly married bride. If a woman died in her matrimonial home within seven years under unnatural or suspicious circumstances, a special legal provision was incorporated which is termed as S.304B – Dowry Death.

If a woman committed suicide due to harassment for dowry within seven years of her marriage, S.306 of IPC-Abetment to Suicide can be invoked.

If the woman was harassed for dowry or was treated with cruelty, S.498A can be invoked. In this case, there is no limitation of seven years after marriage. If her stridhan is not returned to her, S.406 can be invoked, along with S.498A.

S.304-B Dowry Death Life Imprisonment 7 years

S.306 Abetment to Suicide 10 Years -----

S.498-A Cruelty to Wives 3 Years -----

S.406 Criminal Misappropriation of Trust 3 Years ----- check

Despite widespread campaigns against dowry and the stringent laws, why has the menace grown? In our society the social status awarded to the girl's family is much lower than that awarded to the groom's family. Since the need to get the daughters married is overwhelming, the bride's family is not able to refuse the demand for dowry at the time of marriage. They fear that if they don't give dowry, their daughters won't get married. So the parents of the bride prefer to meet the demands of the groom's family in order to get their daughters married, as having an unmarried daughter at home is considered a social stigma.

What is the remedy?

The problem is not with the gifts which are given to the bride from her parents or from her husband's family. The problem is that the woman does not have control over these items and they are considered as the property of the husband and his family. This attitude must be changed. Girls must be advised that the gifts given at the time of marriage are her exclusive property and if she has been forced to leave the matrimonial home due to domestic violence, she has a right to take these with her.

What precautionary measures must be taken at the time of marriage?

The girl's parents must take the following precautions at the time of their daughter's marriage to secure her future:

The girl and her family members must refuse the marriage proposal from a groom or his family members if they make demands for dowry at the time of marriage negotiations. The parents are free to give gifts to their daughter at the time of marriage out of love and affection for her. The gifts given by relatives, friends and even by the husband or his relatives belong exclusively to the bride, and constitutes her stridhan. A list of these gifts received at the time of marriage must be made and the bride, the groom and their parents must sign this document and it must be kept safely with the girl's family or a trusted friend, so that there is no dispute regarding the gifts received as stridhan later. If after the marriage is arranged, valuables or cash is demanded as dowry or gifts, the marriage preparations must be stopped and a complaint under the Dowry Prohibition Act must be immediately be registered. (See the later section regarding property rights of women for a further discussion on this issue.) Rather than cash gifts, relatives must be encouraged to give cheques in favour of the girl at the time of marriage and this should be deposited either in her own separate account or in a joint account in the name of the bride and the groom. All valuables and jewellery which belongs to the bride must be kept in a locker which is in her exclusive name or which is in the joint names of herself and the groom, which she has the right to operate. If after marriage the girl is harassed for more dowry, she must communicate this to her parents through letters or emails. The parents of the girl may meet the groom and his family members to sort out the differences and if they cannot be resolved, the girl must be given a choice to return to her parents' home. In the event that the bride is thrown out of her matrimonial home, she must take with her all her jewellery and valuables. In case this is not possible, at the time of leaving or soon thereafter, she must lodge a complaint to the police mentioning the fact of harassment for dowry and also give the police a list of valuables that are left behind in the husband's home. The police can register a case under the Dowry Prohibition Act as well as under S.498A and S.406 of IPC and help the girl to immediately retrieve her belongings and valuables from the husband's residence. (These IPC provisions are discussed later in this section.) If at this stage no compromise is possible the girl can also initiate proceedings under the Domestic Violence Act for her civil rights such as maintenance, residence, return of belongings, etc.

What is Stridhan?

The gifts given to the bride out of love and affection by her parents or relatives constitute her stridhan. The gifts given to the bride by her husband and/or his relatives also constitute her stridhan. The term—Stridhan means a woman's property and she has exclusive control over it.

Even if it is kept with her husband or his parents, when a woman demands it, it must be given back to her.

How can a woman claim her Stridhan if it is in the possession of her husband or in-laws?

In many families, the stridhan property is kept in the custody of the mother-in-law or the husband. If they refuse to give it back to her, when she demands, or when she is leaving the matrimonial home, it is an offence under S.406 of IPC - **Criminal Misappropriation of Trust**. If the woman lodges a complaint with the police, the police will immediately call the husband/his family members to the police station and request them to return the jewellery and valuables.

If they refuse, the police will file a case under S.406 of IPC and arrest them and also get an order to search and seize the valuables from the premises or bank lockers, etc.

What is cruelty to a wife under the Criminal Law?

Section 498A of IPC defines cruelty as follows: If a husband or his relatives, harass a woman for dowry, or cause any physical or mental harassment which causes harm to her life, limb or sanity, it amounts to cruelty. Is it a serious offence? Yes. It is a serious offence. Though the maximum punishment is only three years, the offence is cognizable, non-bailable and non-compoundable. The police have the power of immediate arrest, even without a court warrant. This causes a great deal of humiliation to the husband and his family members. Once filed, the complaint cannot be withdrawn easily. It can only be quashed by the High Court. Once a complaint under this section is filed, it is difficult to reconcile the marriage.

Can this section be used to address general physical and mental cruelty inflicted on a married woman?

Yes. This section can be used for dowry related harassment as well as for any physical or emotional harassment caused to the wife as it can be seen from the definition of this provision. Section 498-A: Husband or relatives of husband of a woman subject her to cruelty. Whoever, being husband or the relative of the husband of a woman, subjects such women to cruelty shall be punished with imprisonment for a term which may extend to three years and shall also be liable to fine.

Explanation - for the purpose of this section

'Cruelty' means (a) any willful conduct which is of such a nature as is likely to drive the woman to commit suicide or to cause grave injury or danger to life, limb or heath, whether mental or physical of the woman; or (b) harassment of the woman where such harassment is with a view to coercing her or any person related to her to meet any unlawful demand for any property or valuable security or on account of failure by her or any person related to her to meet such a demand.

What are the problems faced by women to register cases under this Section?

Usually the police refuse to register cases under this section unless specific allegations of dowry demands are included in the complaint. But now slowly this misconception is changing. But even now, the police do not register the case straight away. The couple is first sent for counseling, and the police only registers the complaint if the dispute is not resolved. How can cruelty be proved? Cruelty can be proved in various ways such as complaints to the police, medical records, letters written to her parents by the girl, phone calls, phone messages, statements of friends or neighbours, etc.

Is forced sex in marriage (marital rape) within the purview of this section?

Yes, forced sex amounts to sexual violence and is included within the term,—cruelty. So forced sex will come within the purview of this section and if there are any such complaints of this nature, the police must immediately file the complaint and arrest the husband. (though S.498A does not specifically define sexual violence as cruelty, but uses broader general term as 'any physical or mental harassment which causes harm to her life, limb or sanity', rape/sexual violence would come within its scope.)

Rape and Sexual Offences under IPC

(As Amended by the Criminal Law Amendment Act, 2013) Mathura, the catalyst of the anti-rape campaign in India)

Mathura, a 16-year-old poor, orphan, illiterate tribal girl, was raped by two policemen within a police compound in Desai Ganj, a small village in

Chandrapur district of Maharashtra. She was brought to the police station in the evening of 26 March, 1972 on a complaint filed by her own brother that she had eloped with her lover. At 10.00 p.m. at night, while her relatives were waiting outside, after the interrogation, two policemen on duty, Tukaram and Ganpat, took her to a toilet within the compound of the police station and raped her. When the relatives called out to her, she came out in a distorted state with a torn saree and informed them that the policemen had raped her. Hearing the commotion, people gathered and due to their pressure a case of rape was registered. The medical report revealed that there were no marks of injury on her body and that the vagina admitted two fingers easily, which implied that she was habituated to sexual intercourse. Her age was stated as being between 14 and 16 years. The sessions judge, Chandrapur, on 1 June, 1974 acquitted the policemen on the ground that since there were no marks of injury, Mathura must have consented. He labelled her a—shocking liar whose evidence was filled with falsehood.

The judge concluded that though sexual intercourse with the policemen was proved, there was a world of difference between—sexual intercourse and rape.

In an appeal, based on the same evidence, the Nagpur Bench of the Bombay High Court reversed the judgment and convicted the accused to rigorous imprisonment for five years and held that passive or helpless surrender induced by threats or fear cannot be equated with free consent.

However, in an appeal, the Supreme Court, in September, 1978, reversed this judgment, upheld the judgment of the Sessions Court and acquitted the accused on the ground that absence of injuries implies consent. The judgment shocked some law teachers, who wrote an open letter to the Chief Justice of India condemning it as they felt it would snuff out all hopes of justice for millions of Mathura's in the country in 1979. This open letter gave birth to the anti-rape campaign in India and resulted in amendments to the rape laws in 1983.

An important aspect of the amendment was that custodial rape (rape in police custody, prisons, etc.) was made into an aggravated form of sexual crime warranting severe punishment of a minimum of 10 years. The Supreme Court ruling had highlighted the fact that in a rape trial it is extremely difficult for a woman to prove that she did not consent beyond all reasonable doubt as was required under the criminal law. The major demand of the campaign was that the onus of proving consent should shift from the prosecution to the accused. Accordingly, the burden of proof regarding consent was shifted for cases of custodial rape. Since then there have also been several changes in criminal procedures, police manuals, etc. which have given strict guidelines that women cannot be arrested at night and that they cannot be retained in police custody at night.

Definitions of 'sexual offence' under the Indian Penal Code (IPC)

Outraging modesty S. 354 states that if a man assaults or uses criminal force on any woman with the intention of outraging her modesty or knowing that it is likely to outrage her modesty, then he shall be punished under this section.

Sexual Harassment S. 354A states that if a man makes physical contact and advances, demands or requests for sexual favours, shows pornography against the will of a woman or makes sexually coloured remarks, then he shall be punished under this section.

S. 354B states that if a man assaults or uses criminal force against a woman with the intention of disrobing her or compels her to be naked, he shall be punished under this section.

Voyeurism S. 354C states that if a man watches or captures the image of a woman in a private act or disseminates such an image, he shall be punished under this section. A private act includes an act where the victim does not expect to be observed by the man or any other person at his behest. If the victim consents to the capture of the image but not to dissemination, then such dissemination shall be punishable.

Stalking S. 354D states that if a man follows or contacts (or attempts) a woman despite a clear indication of disinterest by her, or monitors the use of internet, email or other electronic communication by her, then he shall be punished under this section.

Rape S. 375 includes: Penetration of the penis, to any extent, into the vagina, mouth, urethra or anus of a woman or if he makes her to do so with him or any other person; or insertion to any extent, any object or a part of the body other than the penis, into the vagina, the urethra or anus of a woman or if he makes her to do so with him or any other person; or manipulation of any part of the body of a woman so as to cause penetration into the vagina, urethra, anus or any body part or if he makes her do so with him or any other person; or If he applies his mouth to her vagina, anus, urethra or makes her to do so with him or any other person.

The above acts amount to rape if they are committed without the consent and against the will of the woman. Even if the consent of the woman is given to the above acts, it will amount to rape under the following circumstances: When consent has been obtained by putting her or any person in whom she is interested, in fear of death or hurt. When the man knows that he is not her husband and she gives consent because she believes him to be her husband. When she is unable to understand the nature and consequence of the act to which consent is given due to intoxication, administration of any stupefying or wholesome substance or due to certain mental unsoundness wherein she is unable to understand the act to which she gives her consent.

S. 376 (2) states that under the following circumstances the offence of rape shall also be committed and the punishment prescribed for the same is more stringent by police officers, by public servants, by armed forces, by management or staff of a jail, remand home, women or children's institute, by management or staff of hospitals, by a relative, guardian or teacher or a person in a position of trust and authority. During communal or sectarian violence rapes a woman, knowing her to be pregnant, rapes a woman below 16 years, rapes a woman who is incapable of giving consent, rapes a woman over whom he is in a position of control or dominance causes grievous bodily harm, maims, disfigures, endangers the life of the woman, rapes her repeatedly, injury which causes the death of the woman or causes the woman to be in a persistent vegetative state.

S.376A states that during the commission of the offence of rape, if a man inflicts an injury which causes the death of the woman or causes the woman to be in a persistent vegetative state, then such an act shall be punishable with a stringent punishment.

Sexual intercourse by husband upon his wife during separation

S. 376B states that if a husband, living separately (with or without a decree of separation) from his wife has sexual intercourse with his wife, without her consent shall be punished with a stringent punishment.

Sexual intercourse by a person in authority

S. 376C states that if a man who is in a position of authority or fiduciary relationship with a woman or public servant or superintendent /manager of a jail, remand home or other place of custody or management/staff of a hospital, abuses his position or seduces a woman under his charge or in his premises to have sexual intercourse with him, then he shall be punished for the offence of rape, with a stringent punishment.

Gang Rape S. 376D states that whenever a woman is raped by two or more persons constituting a group or acting in furtherance of a common intention, then each person is said to have committed the offence of rape and shall be liable to be punished with a stringent punishment.

Repeat Offenders S. 376E states that if a man has been previously convicted for an offence under Ss. 376, 376A or 376D then such person shall be punished with a stringent punishment.

Word, gesture or act intended to insult the modesty of a woman

S. 509 states that if a man utters any word, sound, gesture, exhibits any object with the intention that it is heard or seen or intrudes the privacy of a woman, then he shall be punished under this section.

Abetment and Attempt to commit the above offences is also punishable and is covered above. Confidentiality is to be maintained by Media.

It shall not be lawful for any person to print or publish any matter in relation to proceedings under Ss. 376, 376A, 376B, 376C, 376D, 376E except with the previous permission of the Court. S. 327 (3) Cr.PC. Addressing Biases, Clearing Misconceptions and Understanding Precautionary Measures, "It is not your fault." In our society, if a woman or child is raped, she is treated as an accused and made to suffer. She is made to feel that it is her own fault that she got raped. Her character, conduct, the way she dresses, her past sexual history, etc. become suspected and she is blamed for the crime that is committed on her. Due to the stigma attached to rape, the family is afraid of reporting it to the police. There is also the fear that reporting the crime will diminish the chances of the girl getting married and that the entire family will be humiliated and ostracized.

This is all the more true if the girl is poor or from a backward caste. Hence as change agents it is important for us to spread the message that it is not the fault of the victim that she is raped. If we are aware of our rights, understand the procedures and take precautions, the trauma faced by a victim/survivor during investigation and trial of a rape case will be reduced.

Preserve all evidence: As far as possible, the victim should not have a bath or wash herself or wash the clothes that she was wearing at the time of the offence. It is very difficult to do this because the natural instinct after rape is to clean one's self and also wash the clothes to wipe out the feeling of violation that the offence of rape brings about. The place where the crime was committed also must not be disturbed. This is important to collect the evidence to prove rape.

Do not delay filing the FIR: Due to the stigma attached to the offence, the family takes time to consider whether to report the offence to the police or to hush up the matter. There are several levels of consultations take place within the family and even at the community level. The social status of the rapists or his connection with authorities also matter. If the rapist is wealthy, or has high social standing, and the victim is from a poor family, there will be a great reluctance to report the crime. Similarly if he is a relative or a neighbor, there will be reluctance. Due to this sometimes cases are filed even after many days.

Anyone can get raped. It can happen anywhere – There is a general belief that rape is committed only by strangers in lonely places and dark corners. But the statistics of Maharashtra for 2012 reveal that 94% of the reported cases are by known persons. Fathers, step-fathers, uncles, grandfathers, brothers, brother-in-law, other relatives, neighbors, teachers, doctors, police, boyfriends, his friends, etc. are known to commit rape. Even (husband's commit rape, but this does not get recorded as rape, but it can be filed as an offence under S.498-A IPC - cruelty to wives – discussed later in the next session.) All rapes are not violent specially those committed by known persons. Many times the fact that a young girl is raped is detected only when she is about 5-6 months pregnant. When she approaches the hospital to find out why she has missed her menstrual period, the fact that the child is raped is detected. So be alert.

Penetration by penis into vagina is not important to prove rape: After the recent amendment to rape laws, it is not important to prove penetration of the penis into the vagina. All other sexual activity such as inserting fingers, or objects such as rods, sticks, etc. into the vagina, anus or inserting penis into anus or mouth (oral sex) also constitutes rape. (The legal definitions are discussed in detail later) The victim need not go to the police station to lodge FIR, a relative, friend or social worker can lodge it: The victim may be traumatized after the rape or she may be injured or she may be very scared to go to the police station and narrate the incident to the police.

Remember – there is no need for a victim to go to a police station personally to lodge the FIR. It can be lodged by any person on her behalf. This is the law and you must insist that the police will follow this and not force the victim to come to the police station to lodge the FIR if she is reluctant to do so Her statement can be recorded later at her home or any other place where she is comfortable.

Creating Awareness about Sexual Offences: The new amendment to rape laws have listed out many types of sexual offences and mentioned different body parts. We must also familiarize ourselves with pronouncing the names sexual organs such as i.e. breasts, vagina, buttocks, thighs, anus, penis, etc.. We usually feel embarrassed to utter these words and there is a cultural barrier against naming sexual organs. But under the new law it is very important to describe the offence accurately by naming the concerned body part while recording an FIR. We cannot use general terms such as **izzat loota or galat kaam kiya**. We should also teach our children to be aware of their body parts, and how to protect themselves against sexual abuse and give confidence to them to report it to their care-takers (teachers, parents, etc.) when they are sexually abused. Only then will the stigma attached to rape will be reduced.

Respect the sexual choices made by young women: Many times when a young girl has an affair with a boy and the parents do not approve of it, the girl runs away with the boy. Although the parents are aware that the girl has gone with her own choice, they file a complaint against the boy for kidnapping and rape and get him arrested.

When the girl is brought back she is pressurized into accepting the wishes of the parents and agrees to marry the boy of her choice. Sometimes the girl refuses to accept the choice of their parents and insists on marrying the boy of her own choice and prefers to stay at a shelter home until she becomes major and is able to marry the boy. Such cases tend to get categorized as—false cases through no fault of the girl and due to this all girls become suspect when they wish to file a case of rape. So avoid filing such cases. This defeats the purpose for which we are all fighting - to protect the dignity of women.

A scheme for financial assistance and other support to rape victims: Recently the National Legal Services Authority has drafted a comprehensive scheme for compensation to rape survivors. All state governments are bound to adopt the scheme drafted by **Central Government Support to Victims during Investigation and Trial:**

After recent amendments, a government official can be designated as a support person to help the victim during the procedures of investigation and trial. This person can be a government officer from the Department of Women and Child Development or an NGO member working with the government. The victim can also have her own lawyer. If she has no financial resources, she can ask the state to provide her a lawyer from the legal aid panel.

Case Related to Rape Laws

AK Chopra's Case

Apparel Export Promotion Council vs. AKChopra case, is the first case in which the Supreme Court applied the law laid down in Vishaka's case and upheld the dismissal of a superior officer of the Delhi based Apparel Export Promotion Council who was found guilty of sexual harassment of a subordinate female employee at the place of work on the ground that it violated her fundamental right guaranteed by Article 21 of the Constitution.

In both cases the Supreme Court observed, that, " In cases involving Human Rights, the Courts must be alive to the International Conventions and Instruments as far as possible to give effect to the principles contained therein - such as the **Convention on the Eradication of all Forms of Discrimination Against Women, 1979 [CE DAW]** and the **Beijing Declaration** directing all state parties to take appropriate measures to prevent such discrimination."

The guidelines and judgments have identified sexual harassment as a question of power exerted by the perpetrator on the victim. Therefore, sexual harassment in addition to being a violation of the right to safe working conditions, is also a violation of the right to bodily integrity of the woman.

In Mohd.Habib vs State,

The Delhi High Court allowed a rapist to go scot-free merely because there were no marks of injury on his penis which the High Court presumed was a indication of no resistance. The most important facts such as the age of the victim (being seven years) and that she had suffered a ruptured hymen and the bite marks on her body were not considered by the High Court. Even the eye-witnesses who witnessed this ghastly act, could not sway the High Courts judgment.

The Supreme Court has in the case of **State of Maharashtra vs. Madhukar N. Mardikar,** held that:

The unchastity of a woman does not make her open to any and every person to violate her person as and when he wishes. She is entitled to protect her person if there is an attempt to violate her person against her wish. She is equally entitled to the protection of law. Therefore merely because she is of easy virtue, her evidence cannot be thrown overboard.

MEDICAL TERMINATION OF PREGNANCY ACT

Background of the Act

The MTP Act, passed by the Parliament in 1971 to permit legalized abortions. Prior to 1971, abortion was criminalized under Section 312 of the Indian Penal Code, 1860, except in cases where the procedure was necessary to save the woman's life. The Shah Committee, appointed by the Government of India, carried out a comprehensive review of socio-cultural, legal and medical aspects of abortion, and in 1966 recommended legalizing abortion to protect women's health and lives on both compassionate and medical grounds. It was also viewed as a population control measure.

The term—Medical Termination of Pregnancy(MTP) was used to counter opposition from socio-religious groups who were averse to abortion. How are womens reproductive rights protected? Women's reproductive rights are protected under the Constitution. The right to live under Article 21 include the right to live in dignity which is inclusive of women's reproductive rights (i.e. the right to become pregnant, to bear children, to decide the number of children, the right to have an abortion, to use or not use contraceptives, to be or not to be sterilized, to be or not to be a parent, etc.). A mother's right to preserve her own health is superior to the right of an unborn child.

Do women in India have a right to a legal abortion?

Yes, women in India do have the right to legal abortion. In many countries women had to struggle very hard to get this right. But in India, a law was passed in 1971, the Medical Termination of Pregnancy (MTP) Act to secure for women the right to have legal and safe abortions in public hospitals. This was done to curb the practice of illegal abortions which were carried on rampantly by non-medical professionals at a great risk to women's health.

What is an abortion?

Abortion is a medical procedure of removing the foetus from the uterus of a woman who is pregnant if she wishes not to have the child. This procedure must be carried out only by registered medical practitioners who are authorized to do it under the MTP Act and if not done in a proper condition it poses a risk to the woman's life.

What are the conditions under which a pregnancy can be terminated?

Pregnancy can be terminated in the first trimester (within 12 weeks) if a doctor is of the opinion that it is safe for the woman to undergo an abortion. Beyond 12 weeks and up to 20 weeks, the opinion of two doctors is required to perform the abortion. Beyond that a pregnancy cannot be terminated as it is very risky and may cause harm or even death to the pregnant mother. Hence, it can be performed only in an extreme situation when it is necessary to abort the foetus to save the life of the mother.

[S.3 (2) (a and b)] While deciding whether or not to perform the abortion, the doctors must ascertain the risk of harm to the health of the pregnant mother. The doctors' permission to perform the abortion must be recorded in writing.

Whose consent is required for terminating pregnancy?

If the woman is a major, i.e. above 18 years, she can consent to the abortion herself. If it is a child below 18 years or the person is incapable of giving valid consent (if the person is of unsound mind) the consent of the guardian is required. The consent of the husband is not required to undergo an abortion.

Can the authorities disclose information about the woman who undergoes abortion under the Act?

No, the doctors or the hospital authority cannot disclose to the public any information about the woman who undergoes termination of her pregnancy. This information has to be kept confidential. [S.7 (1) (c)]

Pre-Conception and Pre-Natal Diagnostic Techniques (Regulation) Act (PCPNDT) 1994

Why is the female foetus aborted in our society?

Indian society carries within it a tradition of male preference. The great urge to have boys coupled with a high cost of living has led to a rise in sex-selective abortions. Unfortunately, provisions of the MTP Act are frequently abused in that many families invoke the Act to help them in carrying out abortions of female fetuses after conducting tests to determine the sex of the child using modern technology such as sonography. The age old preference to have sons received a new boost due to this and gradually resulted in a skewed sex ratio. This Act was amended in 2002 and even pre-conception techniques used/ advertised to select the sex of the foetus even before conception was banned. What has the government done to curb this trend? In order to curb this trend, in 1994, Government passed a new **law, known as the Pre-Conception and Pre-Natal Diagnostic Techniques (Regulation and Prevention of Misuse) Act, 1994 (PCPNDT Act for short).**

Since these tests are important to detect foetal abnormalities and genetic defects the tests could not be banned, they could only be regulated. Now the tests can be done only under very strict conditions and they cannot be used for the purpose of identifying and disclosing the sex of the unborn foetus. In order to curb the practice, it has now become necessary to register all sonography machines and also necessary to display very clearly that the hospital or the clinic does not disclose the sex of the unborn foetus.

What is the punishment for misusing the provisions of this Act?

Performing such tests is punishable by up to 3 years of imprisonment and a fine of up to Rs.10,000/- for the first offence and upto five years of imprisonment and a fine of up to Rs. 50,000/- for the subsequent offence. Any doctor doing such a test is also liable to have his license for medical practice suspended for two years for the first offence and permanently after the second offence. (S.23).

Monitoring of Genetic Counseling Centres

The PCPNDT Act provides for regulation of genetic counseling centers, genetic laboratories and genetic clinics and also regulates pre-natal diagnostic procedures. The medical professional running the genetic center has to be registered under the PCPNDT.

Act. 1 It allows the use of prenatal diagnostic techniques for the purpose of specific genetic abnormalities or disorders only and to put down a prohibition on the use of these techniques for determining the sex of the foetus by any such person.

Act. 2 The Act also prohibits any kind of advertisements on pre-conception and pre-natal sex determination of foetus or sex selection of foetus is prohibited.

Act 3 representatives of women's welfare organization to exercise the power and performs the functions conferred on the board under the Act

What are the regulations applied on these centers?

The regulations applied on these centers are as follows:

1. No Genetic Counseling Centre, Genetic Laboratory or Genetic Clinic unless registered under this Act, shall conduct or associate with, or help in, conducting activities relating to pre-natal diagnostic techniques;

2. No Genetic Counseling Centre, Genetic Laboratory or Genetic Clinic shall employ or cause to be employed any person who does not possess the prescribed qualifications;

3. No medical geneticist, gynecologist, pediatrician, registered medical practitioner or any other person shall conduct or cause to be conducted or aid in conducting by himself or through any other person, any pre-natal diagnostic techniques at a place other than a place registered under this Act.

Is there any provision where this genetic counseling centers need to be registered?

Yes, all the genetic centers need to be registered under section please check No person shall open any Genetic Counseling Centre, Genetic Laboratory or Genetic Clinic, including clinic, laboratory or center having ultrasound or imaging machine or scanner or any other technology capable of undertaking determination of sex of foetus and sex selection, or render services to any of them, after the commencement of the Pre-Natal Diagnostic Techniques (Regulation and Prevention of Misuse) Amendment Act, 2002 unless such Centre, Laboratory or Clinic is duly registered under the Act.

Is any person given authority to select the sex of the foetus?

No person can select the sex of the foetus 3A. Prohibition of sex selection. No person, including a specialist or a team of specialists in the field of infertility, shall conduct or cause to be conducted or aid in conducting by himself or by any Kanpur person, sex selection on a woman or a man or on both or on any tissue, embryo, conceptus, fluid or gametes derived from either or both of them please check matter

What are the authorities which control the function of this genetic counseling centers?

The Central Government shall constitute a Board to be known as the **Central Supervisory Board** to exercise the powers and perform the functions conferred on the Board under this Act. The Board shall have the following functions, namely:—

1. to advise the Central Government on policy matters relating to use of pre-natal diagnostic techniques, sex selection techniques and against their misuse;

2. review and monitor implementation of the Act and rules made thereunder and recommend to the Central Government changes in the said Act and rules;

3. to create public awareness against the practice of pre-conception sex selection and pre-natal determination of sex of foetus leading to female foeticide;

4. to lay down code of conduct to be observed by persons working at Genetic Counseling Centres, Genetic Laboratories and Genetic Clinics;

5. to oversee the performance of various bodies constituted under the Act and take appropriate steps to ensure its proper and effective implementation;

Is there any search and seize provision under the Act?

Yes, there is provision under section 30: (1) If the Appropriate Authority has reason to believe that an offence under this Act has been or is being committed at any Genetic Counseling Centre, Genetic Laboratory, Genetic Clinic or any other place, such Authority or any officer authorized in this behalf may, subject to such rules as may be prescribed, enter and search at all reasonable times with such assistance, if any, as such Authority or officer considers necessary, such Genetic Counseling Centre, Genetic Laboratory, Genetic Clinic or any other place and examine any record, register, document, book, pamphlet, advertisement or any other material object found therein and seize and seal the same if such Authority or officer has reason to believe that it may furnish evidence of the commission of an offence punishable under this Act.

(2) The provisions of the Code of Criminal Procedure, 1973 (2 of 1974) relating to searches and seizures shall, so far as may be, apply to every search or seizure made under this Act.

V. Women's Rights under Labour Laws

Introduction

The Constitution of India mandates that women must be treated as equals and prohibits any discrimination against women in all areas, including education, vocational training, skill development and employment. In order to ensure that women get a fair and adequate opportunity of employment, the constitution also mandates reservation for women in educational institutions and in employment in the public sector. Our Constitution also protects the rights of women workers by ensuring that their health and safety is duly protected in the course of employment, particularly those of pregnant women and breast feeding mothers.

The Constitution also safeguards the dignity of women workers and ensures that they are provided a safe working environment free of sexual harassment. In order to fulfill the Constitutional mandate all labour laws contain special provisions regarding the health and safety of women workers by regulating their working hours and by reducing the burden women have to carry. In order to ensure equality the law also mandates that both men and women will be paid the same wages for the same or similar type of work. Recently, a special law has been enacted to protect women against sexual harassment at the workplace. The rights of women under different labour laws are discussed in this section.

Special Protection to Women under the Labour Laws What are the special laws which are enacted to provide adequate protection to women workers? The following laws are specially enacted to provide further protection to women workers:

> The Equal Remuneration Act;

> The Maternity Benefits Act; and

> The Protection of women from Sexual Harassment Act.

> > (Also included is the Minimum Wages Act)

They are applicable only to women and have been enacted to provide special protection and safety for the special needs of women. Does enacting special law for women amount to discrimination? No, enacting special laws for women does not amount to discrimination. The power to enact special laws for women is given to the legislature under Article 15 (3) of the Constitution which stipulates that providing for additional safeguards to women is not discriminatory but will enhance the principle of equality, as it will help women to overcome the wrongs they have suffered for centuries.

12. Equal Remuneration Act,

1976 How does the Equal Remuneration Act safeguard women's rights?

Under the provisions of this Act, every employer is under a legal obligation to pay the same wages for men and women if they perform the same work or work of a similar nature. Even if it is being performed at different places, the salary has to be the same. An employer cannot discriminate against women while recruiting unless employment of women is prohibited or restricted by law. Thus, in matters of recruitment, promotions, training and transfer, the employer is prohibited from discriminating against women.

Who is responsible for ensuring that the provisions of the Act are strictly followed?

The responsibility of ensuring that the provisions of the Act are strictly followed and also that there is no discrimination between men and women in the sphere of recruitment, promotions and training lies with the employer. It is also the responsibility of the employer to maintain proper registers, documents or muster rolls, etc. which can be scrutinized by the labour officer of the district. Any woman who faces discrimination in these aspects can file a complaint before the labour officer of her area.

13. Maternity Benefits Act 1961
Background of the Act

A Maternity Benefits Act stipulates that every woman shall be entitled to, and her employer shall be liable for, the payment of maternity benefit, which is the amount payable to her at the daily wage rate for the period of her actual absence. There is need for maternity benefits so that a woman is able to give quality time to her child without having to worry about whether she will lose her job and her source of income.

This Act was enacted on 12th December 1961, to regulate the employment of women in a certain establishment for a certain period before and after childbirth and to provide for maternity benefit and certain other benefits.

Why maternity leave is important for any women employee?

Women's ties with pregnancy and child-rearing and the failure of employers and policy-makers to deal consistently with this issue exacerbate the difficulties women face in the economy. Women continue to have the primary responsibility for housework and childcare, even when they have extremely demanding jobs. Employers provide help with childcare, flexible work hours to accommodate children's needs, or paid maternity leaves. Women in blue-collar work as well as clerical jobs face rigid time schedules, low pay, and virtually no recognition or help from employers for their family responsibilities Are all establishments included by government? All the establishments are included by government which is under government authority or not. The benefit of the act is provided to all establishment be it mining, plantation and factory. This establishment also includes that all the persons are employed for the exhibition of equestrian, acrobatics and other performances.

How are leaves provided under this act?

Maternity Benefit Act 1961 Leave is granted 26 weeks not more than 8 weeks Remuneration Average daily wage shall be paid for the period of her actual absence immediately preceding and including the day of her delivery and for the six weeks.

Additional Benefits

1. Medical Bonus – 3,500 rupees if no pre-natal confinement and post-natal care is provided for by the employer free of charge;

2. Nursing Breaks; Crèche Facilities; and

3. Four visits a day to the crèche, including the interval for rest

Does the act apply to miscarriage and mother adopting a child also?

In case of miscarriage, a woman shall, on production of such proof as may be prescribed, be entitled to leave with wages at the rate of maternity benefit for a period of six weeks immediately following the day of her miscarriage. In case of the mother adopting child below age of three months shall be provided with leave of 12 weeks. Can any employer dismiss the employ during her leave for pregnancy or deny working from home? Where a woman absents herself from work in accordance with the provisions of this Act, it shall be unlawful for her employer to discharge or dismiss her during or on account of such absence or to give notice of discharge or dismissal on such a day that the notice will expire during such absence, or to vary to her disadvantage any of the conditions of her service. Also with latest amendments a women is allowed to work from home if nature of work is such where women and employee agree on her condition working from home.

Sexual Harassment at Work Place (Prevention, Prohibition and Redressal) Act, 2013

The Sexual Harassment at Workplace Act of 2013 is a special legislation aiming towards providing a safe and hostile free environment at work to women. An effective implementation of the Act will contribute to the realization of their right to gender equality, life and liberty, equality in working conditions everywhere. The sense of security at the workplace will improve women's participation in work, resulting in their economic empowerment and inclusive growth.

The Act is gender-specific to only women.

Evolution: Bhanwari Devi, a social worker from Rajasthan,

During her work, she prevented the marriage of a one-year girl in the community. The issue was reported to the local complaints committee and no action was taken. Bhanwari Devi was however subsequently gang raped by those men.

Vishaka Judgement and SC Guidelines: In the absence of a specific law in India, the Supreme Court, in the Vishaka Judgment, laid down certain guidelines making it mandatory for every employer to provide a mechanism to redress grievances pertaining to workplace sexual harassment.

Who is it Applicable to?

It extends to the whole of India. It applies to both the organised and unorganized sectors in India.

What constitutes "Sexual harassment?

As per the POSCO Act, 'sexual harassment' includes unwelcome sexually tinted behaviour, whether directly or by implication, such as

1. physical contact and advances,

2. demand or request for sexual favours,

3. making sexually coloured remarks,

4. showing pornography, or

5. any other unwelcome physical, verbal or non-verbal conduct of a sexual nature.

Dr. Punita K. Sodhi v. Union of India & Ors. W.P. (C) 367/2009 & CMS 828, 11426/2009 In 2010, the High Court of Delhi upheld the view that sexual harassment is a subjective experience and for that reason held a complete understanding of the complainant's view requires... an analysis of the different perspectives of men and women. Conduct that many men consider unobjectionable may offend many women... Men tend to view some forms of sexual harassment as harmless social interactions to which only overly-sensitive women would object. The characteristically male view depicts sexual harassment as comparatively harmless amusement.... Men, who are rarely victims of sexual assault, may view sexual conduct in a vacuum without a full appreciation of the social setting or the underlying threat of violence that a woman may perceive.

How to Identify "WORK PLACE"?

Work place has to be understood in a wider connotation and not looked in a pedantic approach. **In Saurabh Kumar Mallick v. Comptroller & Auditor General of India**, The word—work place has been objectively defined. The test laid down includes

1. Proximity from the place of work;

2. Control of the management over such a place/residence where the working woman is residing; and

3. Such a residence has to be an extension or contiguous part of the working place.

What are my Reliefs?

The Complainant has the option to file a written complaint to ICC/LCC. Either she can demand an enquiry into the matter or choose to conciliate. In case of the former, the **Complaints Committee** has to conduct a detailed investigation within the workplace and declare their judgement along with the recommendations to the employer. The Complaints Committee has the discretion to suggest the penalties after having heard both the parties. Any aggrieved party also has a right to appeal against the order of the ICC/LCC for further reliefs under this Act.

Where should the complaint be filed?

An important feature of the POSH Act is that it envisages the setting up of a grievance redressal forum.

INTERNAL COMPLAINTS COMMITTEE – ORGANISED SECTOR

The POSCO Act requires an employer to set up an 'internal complaints committee' (ICC) at each office or branch, of an organization employing 10 or more employees, to hear and redress grievances pertaining to sexual harassment.

LOCAL COMPLAINTS COMMITTEE - UNORGANISED SECTOR

At the district level, the Government is required to set up a 'local complaints committee' (LCC) to investigate and redress complaints of sexual harassment from the unorganized sector or from establishments where the ICC has not been constituted on account of the establishment having less than 10 employees or if the complaint is against the employer.

DO'S OF COMPLAINT COMMITTEE/DON'T'S OF COMPLAINT COMMITTEE

1. Use a cheerful, comfortable, airy room for meetings.

2. Ensure that your body language communicates complete attention to the complainant and the accused.

3. Treat the complainant with respect.

4. Discard pre-determined notions of how a victim or accused should look or behave. Beware of stereotypes.

5. All sexual crimes are committed in private, so there may not be any eyewitnesses.

Consult the complainant for:

1. Do not get aggressive.

2. Do not insist on a detailed description of harassment. This could increase the complainant's trauma.

3. Do not allow interruptions during deposition.

4. Do not try and determine the impact of the harassment on the complainant. Let the complainant determine it. Help the complainant, if necessary.

5. Do not discuss the complaint in the presence of others.

6. Remember, this is a human punitive action.

7. If the management does not accept the recommended action, it should give three valid reasons.

8. Help the complainant regain his/her self-respect rights issue, therefore,

   - do not give too much weight age to intention, focus on the impact, and

   - 'proof beyond reasonable doubt' is not required, a strong probability is sufficient.

Minimum Wages Act 1948

Background of The Act:

The Indian Constitution has defined a 'living wage' that is the level of income for a worker which will ensure a basic standard of living including good health, dignity, comfort, education and provide for any contingency. However, to keep in mind an industry's capacity to pay the constitution has defined a 'fair wage'. Fair wage is that level of wage that not just maintains a level of employment, but seeks to increase it keeping in perspective the industry's capacity to pay.

What age group people are allowed to work under labor law?

An adolescent means a person who has completed his/her fourteenth year of age but has not completed eighteenth year and adult means a person who has completed eighteen years. What minimum wages have to be paid?

1. Any minimum rate of wages fixed or revised by the appropriate Government in respect of scheduled employments under section 3 may consist of -

(i)   a basic rate of wages and a special allowance at a rate to be adjusted, at such intervals and in such manner as the appropriate Government may direct, to accord as nearly as practicable with the variation in the cost of living index number applicable to such workers (hereinafter referred to as the cost of living allowance); or

(ii)   a basic rate of wages with or without the cost of living allowance and the cash value of the concessions in respect of supplies of essential commodities at concessional rates, where so authorized; or

(iii)   An all-inclusive rate allowing for the basic rate, the cost of living allowance and the cash value of the concessions, if any. How does government revise the wages and circulate the same detail? The government would revise the wages and circulate in the following manner:

(a) appoint as many committees and sub-committees as it considers necessary to hold enquiries and advise it in respect of such fixation or revision, as the case may be, or

(b) by notification in the Official Gazette, publish its proposals for the information of persons likely to be affected thereby and specify a date, not less than two months from the date of the notification, on which the proposals will be taken into consideration.

What punishments can be imposed upon the employer who has not followed the law under the said act? Any employer who

(a)   pays to any employee less than the minimum rates of wages fixed for that employee's class of work, or less than the amount due to him under the provisions of this Act or

(b)   contravenes any rule or order made under section 13 shall be punishable with imprisonment for a term which may extend to six months or with fine which may extend to five hundred rupees or with both.

Case Related to Right of Women in Labour Law

This was laid down in **Municipal Corporation of Delhi vs. Female Workers (Muster Roll) & Anr.**

In this case, the Municipal Corporation of Delhi granted maternity benefits only to the regular female workers, and denied it to female workers on the muster roll, and not regularised. The Court held that in accordance with Articles 14 and 15 of the Constitution "labour to whichever sector it may belong in a particular region and in a particular industry will be treated on an equal basis."

(Hindustan Antibiotics Ltd. v. Workmen (1967).

Thus, it was held that all women shall be entitled to receive maternity benefits from the establishment.

1. **Payment of Maternity Benefit**: Every woman has the right to be paid maternity benefits from her employer at the rate of her average daily wage, for the entirety of the period wherein she has remained absent from employment, by taking leave in accordance to the provisions of the Act.

2. **Time Period for Maternity Benefit**: The maximum period for which any woman would be eligible to receive such maternity benefit shall be 26 [twenty-six] weeks, of which only a maximum of 8 [eight] weeks can be counted before the date of expected delivery. If a woman has 2 or more surviving children, then the benefit extends to only a period of 12 [twelve] weeks of which a maximum of 6 [six] weeks can be counted preceding her delivery date. In calculating the number of days viable to receive maternity benefit, the Act also includes the holidays as being included in such calculation.

OTHER ACTS 16

The Scheduled Caste and Scheduled Tribes (Prevention of Atrocities) Act

What is the objective of this Act?

It was enacted to prevent the commission of offences of atrocities against the members of Scheduled Castes and Tribes and to provide for Special Courts for the trial of such offences and for the relief and rehabilitation of the victims of such offences. The Act protects the marginalized communities against discrimination and atrocities.

For example, footwear garlands, parading them naked, dumping garbage at premises owned by SC/ST. Further it also provides rehabilitation to the victims of such offences and discrimination by providing an equal opportunity in the field of education and employment. Who can file a complaint? Any scheduled caste or scheduled tribe who is identified accordingly under the law. He/She should be aggrieved and experienced, physical, mental, psychological, emotional or monetary harm or harm to his property as a result of the commission of any discrimination or atrocities. Any relative, legal guardian and legal heirs of the victim are also protected under the law.

What reliefs can be sought?

He/She can be protected from social disabilities such as denial of access to certain public places,

- to use the customary passage without being boycotted,

- personal atrocities like forceful drinking or eating of inedible food,

- sexual exploitation of SC/ST, bodily injury, etc.

One can also be protected from atrocities affecting the properties, malicious prosecution, political disabilities and economic exploitation.

Where can they file a complaint?

The SC and ST Act, 1989 empowers the state government to set up special courts and exclusive special courts in every district to dispose off within 2 months or as far as possible from the date of filing chargesheet. The Act also provides a right to appeal in case of being aggrieved by the order of the Special Court and Exclusive Special Court. The State government also is empowered to ensure effective implementation of the Act.

Protection of witnesses and victims

The SC and ST Act, 1989 has laid down all the rights of the victims and witnesses, in order to curb such violence. It also aims at encouraging its reporting for fair and just implementation of law.

Crimes Against SC and ST: Violence against SC/ST is very nuanced in nature, so it is difficult to separate atrocities against SC/ST from law and order problems. So in many instances, the case is registered under

IPC or CrPC than PoA. Atrocities are in various forms such as cow vigilantism (most dalits are in the occupation of leather making hides of the cow), honour killing, social boycott (Khap Panchayat), caste clashes, discrimination in Universities (Rohit Vemula case). Though the SC/ ST Prevention of Atrocities Act is very stringent, most cases end in acquittal due to police lethargy and due to destruction of evidence of the crime. Also eye-witnesses do not come forward to testify against powerful upper caste men.

Examples of Atrocities in Independent India Kizhavenmani, Tamil Nadu (1958) in which 44 SCs were burnt to death in a confined building because SC agricultural labourers sought a little raise in their very low wages. The High Court acquitted all the accused.

Karamchedu, Andhra Pradesh, 1984: Five SCs were massacred. The trial court convicted many of the accused. The High Court acquitted all. The Supreme Court upheld the trial court judgment – a clear example that acquittals do not mean false cases.

Tsunduru, Andhra Pradesh, 1991: Eight SCs were massacred. The trial court convicted the accused in 2007. The High Court acquitted them in 2014. The Supreme Court has admitted a special leave petition (SLP) of the surviving victims and survivors of victims.

Six cases of Bihar including the Bathani Tola (1996) and Laxmanpur Bathe (1997). In most of these, the trial court convicted the accused. In all of these, the High Court acquitted the accused. Appeals are pending in the Supreme Court, Kambalapalli, Karnataka. The prime witness in this case, who is the sole survivor and head of the family whose other members were massacred, turned hostile due to a threat of life, resulting in the acquittal of all the accused.

Sexual Violence on Dalit Women: Rape, murder and maiming of Dalit women by upper caste men, as retaliation for aspirations of the community for economic and social progress, still continues in the villages and towns of independent India. Lower caste women are raped as part of caste customs and village traditions and are forced to have sex with upper caste landlords and the police. Rape is often used as a form of retaliation to suppress movements demanding payment of minimum wages. These are not isolated incidents but routine occurrences. One hears of several such examples of maintaining the social hierarchy of gendered citizenship. For instance, during the period of 1,300 days from Dec 7, 2003 to June

30, 2007, 1,217 gang rapes were reported in the Madhya Pradesh as per the State Assembly records. Out of these, 362 cases were of women from scheduled castes, 310 were of women from scheduled tribes, and 381 were of women from other backward castes.

An example of this social hierarchy of gendered citizenship through which rights get constituted, is that while the Constitution empowered women through reservations to local panchayats by enacting the 73rd and 74th amendments to the Constitution, newspapers continue to carry reports of Dalit women sarpanches (panchayat heads) being paraded naked and humiliated for holding these positions. Rape of Dalit women continues to be a common occurrence with around 1172 Dalit women having been raped during the year 2005, as reflected in the statistics compiled by the National Crime Record Bureau. Another report revealed that rape of Dalit women in Gujarat rose by 500 per cent since 2001 over the last 13 years, reaching a high point in 2014. While in 2001 only 14 Dalit women reported rape, in 2014 there were 74 Dalit women who reported rape and their cases were registered under the provisions of the Indian Penal Code and Scheduled Castes & Scheduled Tribes (Prevention of Atrocities) Act (popularly referred to as"Atrocities Act').

While most of these violations go unchecked, the gruesome killing of a Dalit woman along with her seventeen-year-olddaughter and two sons, in Khairlanji village in Bhandara district of Maharashtra in September 2006, made national headlines when six people were convicted with death penalty and two with a sentence of life imprisonment by the sessions judge at Bhandara in September, 2008. This was a major landmark victory for Dalit and human rights activists.

Despite this, it is clear that issues concerning both gender and caste were invisibalised in the judicial discourse. As far as caste issues are concerned, the accused were charged with murder under section 302 of the IPC, but were acquitted of charges under Atrocities Act. The activists felt that this glossed over the atrocities committed upon citizens solely due to their caste positions. In August 2010, the Nagpur Bench of Mumbai High Court upheld the Session's Court ruling which had termed the atrocities as mere criminal acts committed out of human rage, leading to a non-application of the provisions of Atrocities Act. The invisibalisation of gender occurred when the courts negated the sexual abuse of the women. Despite the fact that preliminary investigations revealed that the mother, Surekha and the daughter Priyanka were sexually abused prior to their killings, the sexual violence inflicted upon the two women did not receive due judicial recognition both at the Sessions Court as well as the High Court. This despite the fact that the body of Priyanka was found stripped of all clothes. The High Court concluded that since revenge was the motive, there was no intention on the part of the accused to insult the deceased women or to dishonour or outrage their modesty. While both gender and caste were invisibalised, only the crime of murder which comes within the ambit of Section 302 of the IPC was upheld.

While the Sessions Court declared that it was a rarest of rare case warranting death penalty, at the High Court level even the 'rarest of rare' crime was further diluted into an ordinary murder warranting only life imprisonment. As this case highlights, while the sexual brutalities committed on Dalit and tribal women are on the increase, rape and sexual abuse of lower caste and marginalized women are seldom examined within the matrix of the intersectionality of caste and gender. The reported cases constitute only the tip of the iceberg as a large number of cases do not even get recorded. Even those reported and charge-sheeted seldom result in conviction. The Khairlanji verdict is a rare judicial occurrence. A combination of factors contributes to this dismal state of affairs. Non-accessibility of the justice delivery system to marginalised communities due to factors of poverty, illiteracy and fear of the police is one contributory factor. Institutional bias of state agencies against Dalits, leading to biased and callous investigation and prosecution is another. Retraction by eye-witnesses from the higher castes is yet another factor. The caste and gender bias in courts of law is a further contributing factor.

Some landmark Judgement related to women's rights

Voluntary Health Association of Punjab v. Union of India
Supreme Court of India (2013)

Gender Discrimination

The Parliament of India enacted the Pre-Conception and **Pre-Natal Diagnostic Techniques (Prohibition on Sex-Selection) Act of 1994** as a measure of preventing female foeticides and as a form of affirmative action for women and girls to end discrimination against girl children in furtherance of the constitutional principle of equality under Article 15 of the Indian Constitution. The Supreme Court in 2001 and 2003 noticed a lack of effective implementation and misuse of the Act and thus had issued directions to the Union Government and the State Governments for its proper implementation. Having noticed a decline in the female child sex ratio as reported in the 2011 Census, the Court directed personal appearance of the Health Secretaries of the States of Punjab, Haryana, NCT Delhi, Rajasthan, Uttar Pradesh, Bihar and Maharashtra, to examine steps undertaken for effective implementation of the provisions of the Act as well as the various directions issued by the Court. The Court emphasized that women have equal right of thinking, participating and becoming leaders in the society, stating that the purpose of the Act can only be realized when government authorities carry out their functions with commitment and awareness about the role of women in a society. After a detailed analysis of the steps undertaken by the Union and the State Governments, the Court issued directions—including regular monitoring and reporting by authorities under the Act, faster disposal of cases filed under the Act, and suspension of licenses to practice for convicted doctors—to ensure implementation.

Khurana and Others v. Union of India and Others
Supreme Court of India (2014)

Employment Discrimination

The **Cine Costume Make-up Artists and Hair Dressers Association of Mumbai (Association)** was registered as a trade union under the Trade Unions Act, 1926. The Association's by-laws prohibited qualified women make-up artists from becoming members of the Association based solely on their sex. Ms. Charu Khurana, a women make-up artist whose application for membership to the Association was rejected, challenged this prohibition on the grounds that it violated several rights under the Indian Constitution, including her rights to equality, to employment, and to a livelihood. Noting that gender justice is integral to the Indian Constitution, the Supreme Court struck down the Association's by-laws as violating Articles 14, 15 and 21. Although the Court acknowledged that Fundamental Rights in India are enforceable only against the State and its authorities and not against purely private individuals or organizations, it found at the same time that a clause in the by-laws of a trade union registered under the Trade Unions Act, 1926, which is accepted by the Registrar of Trade Unions—a State authority under the Trade Unions Act—cannot violate the Indian Constitution.

Sarma v. V.K.V. Sarma Supreme Court of India (2013)

Domestic and Intimate Partner Violence, Gender Discrimination

Ms. Indra Sarma, an unmarried woman, left her job and began a "live-in" relationship with Mr. V.K.V. Sarma for a period as long as 18 years, despite knowing that he was married. Mr. Sarma abandoned Ms. Sarma in a state where she could not maintain herself. Under the **Protection of Women from Domestic Violence Act, 2005,** failure to maintain a woman involved in a "domestic relationship" amounts to "domestic violence." Two lower courts held that Mr. V.K.V. committed domestic violence by not maintaining Ms. Sarma, and directed Mr. Sarma to pay a maintenance amount of Rs.18,000 per month. Thereafter, on appeal, the High Court of Karnataka set aside the orders of the lower courts on the ground that Ms. Sarma was aware that Mr. Sarma was married and thus her relationship with him would fall outside the protected ambit of "relationship in the nature of marriage" under the Protection of Women from Domestic Violence Act, 2005. On further appeal, the Supreme Court, while affirming the High Court's order, created an exception to the general rule. The Supreme Court clarified that a woman who begins to live with a man who is already married to someone else, without knowing that he is married, will still be considered to be in a "domestic relationship" under the Protection of Women from Domestic Violence Act, 2005; thus, the man's failure to maintain her will amount to "domestic violence" within the meaning of the Act and she will be eligible to claim reliefs such as maintenance and compensation. This case is important because it established for the first time such an exception and calls for legislative action to protect women like Ms. Sarma whose contributions in a joint household are often overlooked.

Hariharan v. Reserve Bank of India Supreme Court of India (1999)

Gender Discrimination

Ms. Githa Hariharan was married to Dr. Mohan Ram and they had a son named Rishab. She applied to the Reserve Bank of India (RBI) for bonds to be held in the name of their minor son Rishab and had signed off as his guardian. The RBI sent back the application to her advising her to either produce the application signed by the father of Rishab or produce a certificate of guardianship from a competent authority in her favor. RBI was of the opinion that Dr. Mohan was the natural guardian of Rishab on the basis of Section 6(a) of the **Hindu Minority and Guardianship Act, 1956 (HMGA).** That provision stated that the father is the natural guardian of a Hindu minor child and the mother is the guardian "after" the father. Ms. Hariharan challenged the constitutional validity of this provision in the Supreme Court on grounds that it violated the right to equality guaranteed under Articles 14 and 15 of the Indian Constitution. The Supreme Court, relying on gender equality principles enshrined in the Indian Constitution, CEDAW and UDHR, widely interpreted the word "after" in the provision and upheld the constitutional validity of Section 6(a) HMGA, 1956. It held that both the father and mother are natural guardians of a minor Hindu child, and the mother cannot be said to be the natural guardian only after the death of the father as that would not only be discriminatory but also against the welfare of the child, which is legislative intent of HMGA, 1956. This case is important because it established for the first time that a natural guardian referred to in the HMGA, 1956 can be a father or a mother: whoever is capable of and available for taking care of the child and is deeply interested in the welfare of the child, and that need not necessarily be the father.

Mohd. Ahmed Khan v. Shah Bano Begum Supreme Court of India (1985)

Divorce and Dissolution of Marriage, Gender Discrimination

Ms. Shah Bano Begum was married to a lawyer named Mr. Mohd. Ahmed Khan. They lived together for 43 years and had five children. In 1978, Mr. Khan threw Ms. Begum out of the shared household and Ms. Begum applied for maintenance from Mr. Khan under Section 125 of the **Criminal Procedure Code, 1973 (Cr.P.C, 1973)**. Pending her application, Mr. Khan dissolved the marriage by pronouncing a triple talaq (divorce on the triple utterance of the word "talaq" by a Muslim husband) and paid Ms. Begum 3000 rupees as **mehr** (money/valuable property promised to a Muslim woman for her financial security under the marriage contract) and a further sum of maintenance for the **iddat** period (a period of 3 months that a Muslim woman has to observe before she can remarry after her divorce). Mr. Khan argued that Ms. Begum's claim for maintenance should be dismissed as Ms. Begum had received the amount due to her on divorce under the Muslim personal law. The lower court granted Ms. Begum's claim for maintenance, which was set at 179 rupees per month by the High Court in a revision application. Mr. Khan appealed to the Supreme Court in 1985 and the Court held that a payment made pursuant to personal laws cannot absolve a husband of his obligation to pay fair and reasonable maintenance under Section 125 Cr.P.C, 1973 and a husband can be liable to pay maintenance beyond the iddat period.

Latifi v. Union Of India Supreme Court of India (2001)

Domestic and Intimate Partner Violence, Gender Discrimination

The **Muslim Women (Protection of Rights on Divorce) Act, 1986 (MWPRDA, 1986)** seemed to overrule the Supreme Court's decision in Mohd. Ahmed Khan v. Shah Bano Begum. Pursuant to a prima facie reading of the MWPRDA, 1986, a Muslim husband was responsible to maintain his divorced wife only for the **iddat** period and after such period the onus of maintaining the woman would shift on to her relatives. The matter resurfaced before the Supreme Court in Danial Latifi v. Union of India when the constitutional validity of the MWPRDA, 1986 was challenged on the grounds that the law was discriminatory and violative of the right to equality guaranteed under Article 14 of the Indian Constitution as it deprived Muslim women of maintenance benefits equivalent to those provided to other women under Section 125 of Criminal Procedure Code, 1973. Further, it was argued that the law would leave Muslim women destitute and thus was violative of the right to life guaranteed under Article 21 of the Indian Constitution. The Supreme Court, on a creative interpretation of the MWPRDA, 1986, upheld its constitutionality. It held that a Muslim husband is liable to make reasonable and fair provision for the future of his divorced wife extending beyond the iddat period. The Court based this interpretation on the word "provision" in the MWPRDA, 1986, indicating that "at the time of divorce the Muslim husband is required to contemplate the future needs [of his wife] and make preparatory arrangements in advance for meeting those needs" (at 11). This case is important because, it established for the first time that a Muslim husband's liability to provide maintenance to his divorced wife extends beyond the iddat period, and he must realize his obligation within the iddat period, thereby striking a balance between Muslim personal law and the Criminal Procedure Code, 1973.

State of Maharashtra v. Indian Hotel & Restaurants Association Supreme Court of India (2013)

Employment Discrimination, Gender Discrimination

The **Bombay Police Act, 1951** was amended in 2005 with the object of securing public order, morality, dignity of women, and reducing exploitation of women including trafficking of minor girls. Section 33A was inserted that prohibited performance of all types of dance in eating houses or permit rooms or beer bars. Section 33B was inserted that permitted three star hotels and Government associated places of entertainment to hold dance performances. The Indian Hotel & Restaurants Association filed a writ petition challenging Section 33A of the Bombay Police Act, 1951 before the Bombay High Court on the grounds that such prohibition: (a) discriminates against women employed to dance in eateries and bars and those employed to dance in three star hotels and government establishments; (b) interferes with their right to work and right to earn a livelihood, and thus is violative of the Indian Constitution. The Bombay High Court held that Section 33A is violative of Articles 14 (equality) and 19(1)(g) (right to work), of the Indian Constitution. The Government of Maharashtra filed an appeal before the Supreme Court and prayed that the terms "All dance" found in Section 33A be read down to mean "dances which are obscene and derogatory to the dignity of women" instead of striking it off altogether to ensure that the right to work of women is not interfered with. The Supreme Court upheld the judgement of the Bombay High Court. It declared that Section 33A violates Article 14 the Constitution of India on the ground that such law is based on an unacceptable presumption that the so-called elite (i.e. rich and the famous) have higher standards of decency, morality or strength of character than their counterparts who have to content themselves with lesser facilities of inferior quality in the dance bars. It declared that Section 33A violates Article 19(1)(g) on the ground that it interferes with the right of women to work and that, contrary to the ban's purpose, it resulted in forcing some women into prostitution. The Court further urged the government to take affirmative action to ensure the safety and improve the working conditions of the persons working as bar dancers who primarily constitute of women.

Bachpan Bachao Andolan v. Union of India & Others
Supreme Court of India (2011)

Trafficking in Persons

Children's' rights, child labor, forced labor, human trafficking, sexual abuse.

Bachpan Bachao Andolan, a non-governmental organization in India submitted a petition to the Supreme Court of India to take action against the use of child performers in India's traveling circuses. A study found that children were being trafficked from Nepal or taken from their homes, exploited as child laborers in these circuses, and subjected to mental, physical, and sexual abuse. In recognition that this practice was in violation of child labor laws and regulations on a child's right to an education, among other national and international statutes, the Supreme Court gave an order to prohibit the employment of children in circuses, raid circuses to free children, and establish rehabilitation schemes for the child victims. This case is an important victory for children's rights in India, where parents often sell their children to work at a young age, and also displays the willingness of the Supreme Court of India to hear petitions from NGOs, offering an important avenue for human rights reform.

Kishangiri Mangalgiri Goswami v. State of Gujarat Supreme Court of India (2009)

Domestic and Intimate Partner Violence, Gender-based Violence in General

A man convicted in part under § 306 of the Indian Penal Code appealed the charge of abetting his wife's suicide. There was a history of dowry-related abuse, and the husband demanded another 40,000 rupees from his wife and her family before the she committed suicide by burning herself. The Court held that cruelty alone was not enough to convict the husband for abetment of suicide. Showing abetment requires proof of direct or indirect acts of instigation, conspiracy or intentional aid. The man's conviction was upheld on other grounds.

D.S. Grewal v. Vimmi Joshi Supreme Court of India (2008)

Employment Discrimination, Gender Discrimination, Sexual Harassment

Vimmi Joshi was the principal of a public school who alleged her superior had sent her love letters and made sexual advances towards her. She brought a complaint to the **School Managing Committee** and was asked to bring the complaint in writing. Subsequently, the Committee received two anonymous complaints against Joshi and her employment was terminated. She challenged the termination claiming sexual harassment. The High Court held that this was a clear case of sexual harassment and ordered disciplinary actions to be taken. The Supreme Court reversed and remanded the High Court's decision because the Supreme Court had previously laid out guidelines for sexual harassment complaints in Vishaka v. State of Rajasthan; a complaint committee must have been formed to inquire into the complaint further. The Supreme Court held that since the High Court did not fully look into the matter, they could not have found that this was a clear-cut case of sexual harassment. The High Court was directed to appoint a three-member committee, which must be headed by a woman, to hear the case.

Shekara vs. State of Karnataka Supreme Court of India (2009)

Sexual Violence and Rape

A man induced a girl to have intercourse with him on a false promise to marry her and then threatened to kill her and her mother. School records showed that the girl was less than 16-years-of age. The Court held the man could not be convicted of rape for his false promise, but he could be convicted for the use of criminal force on a woman with intent to outrage her modesty. This case demonstrates that men can be criminally convicted for lying to a woman in order to have intercourse with her.

Bangaru Venkata Rao v. State of Andhra Pradesh Supreme Court of India (2008)

Domestic and Intimate Partner Violence

A husband killed his wife by stabbing her in the abdomen and was sentenced under **Section 302 of the Indian Penal Code to life imprisonment**. He appealed the sentence, claiming that the record clearly establishes that he only delivered a single blow to his wife in a sudden quarrel, and therefore conviction under Section 302 is not proper. The High Court dismissed the appeal but the Supreme Court reversed, holding that the husband's actions in a sudden fight did not warrant life imprisonment. His sentence should have been brought under the fourth exception of Section 300, accounting for the heat of passion in a sudden fight, and accordingly his sentence was reduced to ten years.

Satyapal v. State of Haryana Supreme Court of India (2009)

Statutory Rape or Defilement

A village man sexually assaulted an 11-year-old girl; he ran away when the girl's aunt approached. In an attempt to avoid the stigma of a sexual attack, her family convened a village panchayat to resolve the dispute. The police were contacted when the panchayat was unsuccessful, and the girl did not have a medical examination until 80 hours after the attack. The exam found vaginal bruising but not penetration. Despite the delays, the Court upheld the conviction under § 376 of the Penal Code. This case is notable because the Court allowed a delay in filing the report and found that full penetration is not necessary for a rape conviction.

Shivaji @ Dadya Shankar Alhat v. The State of Maharashtra Supreme Court of India (2008)

Sexual Violence and Rape, Statutory Rape or Defilement

A man led a nine-year-old girl to a hill where he raped, strangled and murdered her. The girl's sister testified that she saw her sister leave with the man and the mother later recovered the girl's body from the hill and filed a police report against the accused. He was convicted and sentenced to death under Sections 376 and 302 of the Indian Penal Code. The man appealed, claiming that he should not be sentenced to death on circumstantial evidence alone. The High Court dismissed the appeal. The Supreme Court affirmed, holding that circumstantial evidence establishes the guilt of the accused, forming the conviction, but does not bear any relation to the sentencing. The Supreme Court defers discretion to trial judges in arriving at a proper sentence dealing with the subtleties of each case.

State of Rajasthan v. Hemraj & Anr Supreme Court of India (2009)

Sexual Violence and Rape

The Supreme Court held that a woman present for a gang rape did not share the common intention to rape and, therefore, could not be convicted of rape. According to §§ 375 and 376 of the Penal Code, only a man can commit rape, making it impossible for a woman to be convicted of a gang rape. This case is important because it raises the issue of how or when to hold women responsible for sexual violence against other women.

Noorjahan v. State Rep. by D.S.P. Supreme Court of India (2008)

Dowry-related Violence

Shortly after a couple married, the husband and his relatives began treating the wife poorly and demanded dowry from her. The husband and his brother later strangled her with rope and his sisters held the wife's arms. This led to her death. All of the accused were convicted and sentenced under Sections 302 and 498(a) of the Indian Penal Code. The aunt of the husband was also convicted and sentenced under 498(a) for her alleged dowry-related cruelty, which can lead to a sentence of up to three years imprisonment. The aunt appealed her conviction, claiming that if she had been cruel it bore no relation to dowry. The High Court upheld the conviction, yet the Supreme Court reversed. The Supreme Court held that the purpose of Section 498(a) was to combat dowry-related death and cruelty. Because there was no evidence that the aunt had ever made a demand for dowry, rendering her conviction under Section 498 improper.

Rajbir @ Raju & Anr v. State of Haryana Supreme Court of India (2010)

Domestic and Intimate Partner Violence

This case involved an appeal of a man's lifetime imprisonment sentence. He was convicted of murdering his pregnant wife after she asked for money six months after their marriage. The Punjab & Haryana High Court reduced the sentence to 10 years rigorous imprisonment. The man's mother was also awarded two years rigorous imprisonment. While the reduction in the husband's sentence was issued, the Court directed all trial courts in India to ordinarily add § 302 to the charge of § 304B, so that death sentences can be imposed in such heinous and barbaric crimes against women.

State of Rajasthan v. Madan Singh Supreme Court of India (2008)

Sexual Violence and Rape

The trial court convicted a man of raping a ten-year-old girl and sentenced him to ten years of imprisonment under Section 376(2)(f) of the Indian Penal Code. On appeal, the High Court reduced his sentence to seven years considering the convicted had already suffered a custodial sentence of six years, was young, and the only breadwinner in the family with two children. The Supreme Court, however, reversed the High Court's reduction of the sentence because it fell below the statutory minimum. The Supreme Court held that the measure of punishment in a rape case cannot depend on the social status of the victim or the accused. It must depend on the conduct of the accused, the state and age of the victim, and the gravity of the criminal act. Crimes of violence upon women are to be severely dealt with. The proviso to Section 376(2) specifies that the court may, for special and adequate reasons, impose a sentence of less than ten years. However, the Supreme Court in the present case, found there to be no justifiable extenuating or mitigating circumstances available that would justify imposing a less-than-minimum sentence.

Utpal & Anr. v. State of West Bengal Supreme Court of India (2010)

Gender-based Violence in General

On April 28, 1984 four or five men took Ms. Sitarani Jha from a bus stop to a house under construction and two of the men forcibly raped her. The trial court determined that the prosecution had not proven the case beyond a reasonable doubt. The case was appealed and the High Court determined that the defendants were guilty under Section 376/34 of the India Penal Code. The case was brought before the Supreme Court to determine if the High Court erred in finding the appellants guilty of rape, because no physical injuries were found on the private parts of the victim's body. The Supreme Court determined that the High Court did not err. Ms. Sitarani Jha was able to identify her attackers, and that a lack of injuries on the private parts of a rape victim were not enough to acquit an identified rapist.

State of Tamil Nadu vs. Ravi Supreme Court of India (2006)

Gender Violence in Conflict

The High Court reversed the trial court's conviction of a man who had raped a four or five-year-old child. He had penetrated the vagina before two people stopped him. A physical exam showed her hymen was torn. A doctor also found a cut on the man's penis consistent with an injury from forced sex. The Supreme Court reinstated the trial court's conviction. This case is important because the Court stated that a rape conviction could be sustained solely on the basis of testimony of the victim. In addition, the Supreme Court stated that rape victims should not be treated like accomplices in a crime and that their testimony, instead, should be viewed as the testimony of an injured witness. The Supreme Court also stated that the testimony of a rape victim should receive "great weight." In this case, however, the Supreme Court found that there was a great deal of corroborating evidence in addition to the testimony of the victim.

State of Rajasthan v. Jaggu Ram Supreme Court of India (2008)

Dowry-related Violence

A new bride was threatened by her in-laws if her family did not provide a greater dowry. When local villagers protested these threats, the husband's family killed his new bride by burning her with kerosene. The main issue of the case was to determine how the elements of dowry-death should be proven at trial under amended Indian Penal Code. The trial court acquitted the defendant of dowry-death in taking a narrow statutory view. The Supreme Court reversed, holding that a death shall be called dowry-death when a woman dies from burns or bodily injury that would not occur under normal circumstances within seven years of marriage. The Court added it should be in consideration that soon before her death the woman was subject to harassment by her husband or any relative of his or in connection with any demand for dowry. Shifting this burden to the husband's family and broadening the scope of dowry-death provides prosecutors with more powerful tools to convict for dowry-death and is meant to curb the recent rise in dowry-related violence.

Singh v. State of U.P. & Another Supreme Court of India (2006)

Gender-based Violence in General

A man and a woman from different castes married. The woman's brothers objected to the inter-caste marriage and lodged false complaints of criminal activity against the husband and his family. They also alleged the woman was not mentally fit, leading to her committal. The husband's family members filed a petition to the High Court, and the High Court ordered them to appear before a sessions judge who would assess whether they had committed a crime. The family members petitioned the Supreme Court under Article 32 of the Constitution. The Court ended all proceedings pending against the husband's family and the warrants against them. The Court held that the police and administrative authorities have a duty to protect individuals from harassment, threats, and violence based on an inter-caste marriage. In doing so, the Supreme Court stated that the Hindu Marriage Act does not ban inter-caste marriages and admonished violent acts in protest of inter-caste marriages.

Viswanathan v. State Rep. By Inspector of Police Supreme Court of India (2008)

Sexual Violence and Rape

A young woman was returning home from work when she was attacked and raped by a group of men. While the woman was able to identify three of her assailants, due to falling unconscious, she was unsure of who had raped her. No Test Identification Parade was held. Upon examination, she was found with no bodily injuries. The trial court convicted six men finding common intention to commit gang rape. The Supreme Court affirmed in part and reversed in part. Three of the convictions could not be upheld because of the victim's failure to identify them. The significance of this case, however, is the Court's recognition that identifiable physical injury is not necessary to prove rape; the circumstances in which a victim is found can be sufficient. And the recognition that not all of the convicted must have committed the actual rape but need only have the intention to commit gang rape.

Md. Kalam v. The State of Bihar Supreme Court of India (2008)

Sexual violence and Rape, Statutory Rape or Defilement

A man convicted of raping a six-year-old girl appealed his sentence of 10 years, alleging the child's testimony should not have been accepted without corroboration. He also insisted his sentence was too harsh. A child's testimony is acceptable as long as the court carefully evaluates it. Both the trial court and the High Court did this and found the child's evidence reliable. The Supreme Court denied his appeal regarding the girl's testimony but lessened his sentence to 5 years imprisonment with fines.

Golla Yelugu Govindu v. State of Andhra Pradesh Supreme Court of India (2008)

Domestic and Intimate Partner Violence

A fourteen-year marriage broke down when the husband became addicted to "vices"; he began to beat his wife and demanded money from her parents. During a quarrel, with their children in the room, the husband killed his wife by hacking her with a sickle in her back and neck. The trial court convicted him and sentenced him to a life imprisonment, but he appealed, claiming that his children were too young to be competent witnesses. The Supreme Court held that there is no age restriction on competency. All people are competent to testify unless they cannot understand questions or give rational answers. The Supreme Court did reduce his sentence, however, to ten years, because the murder was done in a sudden act and not premeditated.

Moti Lal v. State of M.P Supreme Court of India (2008)

Sexual Violence and Rape

A man raped a woman while she guarded her husband's agricultural field. The woman and her husband filed a police report, and the man was arrested and convicted under §§ 450 and 376(1) of the Indian Penal Code and § 3(1)(xii) of the Scheduled Castes and Scheduled Tribes Prevention of Atrocities Act. The offender appealed his conviction on the grounds that the prosecution relied too heavily on the victim's testimony. The Court denied his appeal. Emphasizing the stigma associated with incidents of rape, the Court reaffirmed Indian courts' presumption that rape victims who file reports are telling the truth.

Sunita Jain v. Pawan Kumar Jain Supreme Court of India (2008)

Domestic and Intimate Partner Violence, Dowry-related Violence

Immediately after a woman's marriage, her husband and his parents harassed her for having an insufficient dowry. She was attacked on two occasions and prevented from seeing her two children. A few years later the husband filed for divorce and the woman filed a police report against her husband and his family for mental torture and dowry demands. The High Court initially allowed the case to continue and then quashed the proceedings and filed a petition against the woman claiming abuse of court. The woman appealed on the question of whether a criminal court can review its prior decisions. The Supreme Court set aside the High Court's petition stating that the court was wrong to quash the woman's proceedings when the High Court initially found that there was a prima facie case against the husband and family. Under the Indian Penal Code, a court does not have the power to alter its prior judgment.

State of Himachal Pradesh v. Raghubir Singh Supreme Court of India (1993)

Sexual Violence and Rape, Statutory Rape or Defilement

While traveling to her house, an 8/9 year-old girl was separated from her father and sister while in her family's fields. The defendant kidnapped and raped her under a nearby mango tree. The Supreme Court reversed the High Court's acquittal and found the defendant guilty of rape. The Supreme Court stated that the conviction could be upheld solely on the victim's testimony, despite her age, if it is believable and there is no evidence to discredit its trustworthiness.

State of Maharashtra v. Kewalchand Jain Supreme Court of India (1990)

Sexual Violence and Rape

A police inspector contrived to have the fiance of a young girl locked up, and after doing so, went to her hotel room and raped her. The Supreme Court refuted the notion that testimony of a victim of sexual violence requires corroboration and found that courts should not be reluctant to accept the evidence of a rape victim, if under the totality of the circumstances appearing on the record of the case the victim does not have a strong motive to lie. A rape victim's evidence is to receive the same weight that would be given to any victim of physical violence. The Supreme Court noted that corroboration of the testimony of a woman who is a victim of sexual violence is not required except in extremely rare circumstances.

State of Orissa v. Naiko Supreme Court of India (1992)

Sexual Violence and Rape

A woman was kidnapped in broad daylight, taken to a forest, then gang-raped. The defense argued that the woman's injuries were not severe enough for her to have resisted multiple rapists. The Court held that a woman need not present evidence of resistance to support a charge of rape.

State of Punjab v. Ramdev Singh Supreme Court of India (2003)

Gender-based Violence in General, Sexual Violence and Rape

A case of sexual assault where the accused was acquitted. The State appealed and the court determined that lack of physical evidence of rape and previous sexual activity on the part of the victim cannot be grounds for acquittal and the court restored the conviction. Also, the testimony need not be corroborated with additional evidence as long as there is an assurance of veracity.

State of West Bengal v. Jaiswal Supreme Court of India (1993)

Domestic and Intimate Partner Violence, Dowry-related Violence, Harmful Traditional Practices

A woman committed suicide by hanging herself after being mistreated and abused by her husband, being subject to complaints about her dowry and held responsible for the death of her father-in-law because of her "evil luck" by her in-laws, and being subjected to other mental torture. In an action against the woman's husband and mother-in-law, the lower court had found insufficient evidence of systematic cruelty or physical or mental torture to sustain a conviction under 498 A of the Indian Penal Code, which provides that a relative of a woman that subjects that woman to cruelty may be imprisoned for up to three years. The Supreme Court reversed the lower court's holding, finding that the actions of the accused husband and mother-in-law did qualify as "cruelty" because their willful conduct was of such nature as was likely to commit the victim's suicide.

The Chairman, Railway Board & ORS v. Mrs. Chandrima Das & ORS Supreme Court of India (2000)

Gender-based Violence in General, Sexual Violence and Rape

A case of gang-rape under public law because the accused were employees of the national railway. The case includes a discussion of the application of UN resolutions domestically, including the **Declaration on the Elimination of Violence against Women and the Universal Declaration of Human Rights.** The Court concludes that the victim can recover under public law due to the violation of her Fundamental Rights, enshrined in the declarations and the Indian Constitution.

Vishaka v. State of Rajasthan Supreme Court of India (1997)

Gender Violence in Conflict, Gender-based Violence in General

This case involved a public interest petition filed by a group of NGOs for enforcement of the Constitution's protection of women's rights and international women's rights norms. The victim was gang-raped and before the rape had complained to the authorities, but there was no response. The court held that 13 is a violation of gender equity and the right to life and liberty and the government must provide safeguards to prevent such harassment from happening.

Shanti v. State of Haryana Supreme Court of India (1991)

Dowry-related Violence, Harmful Traditional Practices

The petitioners were charged and found guilty of dowry death. The Court upheld the conviction, holding that the evidence of cruelty necessary to create a presumption of dowry death may be less than or different from the level of evidence of cruelty necessary to uphold a charge of criminal cruelty. The two crimes are unrelated, despite using similar wordings, and a person may be convicted of dowry death without having committed criminal cruelty.

Smt. Seema v. Ashwani Kumar Supreme Court of India (2007)

Forced and Early Marriage, Harmful Traditional Practices

The Supreme Court ordered that all marriages be registered in order to prevent child marriage.

State of Andhra Pradesh v. Gangula Satya Murthy Supreme Court of India (1996)

Sexual Violence and Rape

The Supreme Court of India found that the High Court had insufficient reason to overturn a rape conviction, holding that rape cases should be tried with the "utmost sensitivity" and the court must look at the "totality of the background" of the case.

Mandal v. Deen Dayal Harinagar Hospital Supreme Court of India (2010)

Gender Discrimination

A public interest litigation was initiated to urge the Indian government to address the issue of high levels of maternal mortality in the country. The Court ordered the government to correct discriminatory actions in programs intended to reduce maternal mortality, to report on what corrective steps will be taken to monitor and improve current programs, and to create additional programs if necessary.

Naz Foundation v. Govt. of Delhi Supreme Court of India (2009)

Gender-based Violence in General, LGBTIQ

A public interest litigation was initiated to change the definition of non-criminal sex from "hetero-sexual penile-vaginal" to "consensual sex between adults." The court granted the petition finding the criminalization of non-heterosexual sex violative of the constitution.

P. Rathinam v. Union of India Supreme Court of India (1994)

Domestic and Intimate Partner Violence

The Supreme Court held that criminal penalties for suicide violate the constitutional right to life by amounting to a double punishment; specifically arguing that women who attempt suicide after abuse cannot be criminally penalized for their suicide attempt. Previously, Indian law carried criminal penalties for attempted suicide.

Pandurang Shivram Kawathkar v. State Of Maharashtra Supreme Court of India (2001)

Dowry-related Violence, Harmful Traditional Practices

The petitioner, having been found guilty under the Dowry Prohibition Act, charged that because the witnesses were all related, their testimony was insufficient to prove that he participated in a demand for dowry. The Court held that the testimony is sufficient to uphold a charge, and that evidence of a demand for dowry having been presented it is up to the defendant to prove that he did not participate in the demand — to prove an alibi.

People's Union for Democratic Rights v. Union of India Supreme Court of India (1982)

Gender Violence in Conflict

In this public interest litigation, the Court reaffirmed that the equal pay for equal work provision of the constitution is valid, and that the employer, whether public or private, is responsible for enforcing it and taking prompt disciplinary action when violations occur.

Prerana v. State of Maharashtra Supreme Court of India (2002)

Sexual Violence and Rape, Trafficking in Persons

After a police raid on a brothel, four pimps were arrested and twenty-four women and girls were taken into custody. The magistrate ordered a medical examination to, among other things, determine the women's ages. The magistrate then ordered that the women 18 and over be released, and a few days later ordered the minor girls to be released. The magistrate explained that the girls had expressed a desire to be released. The Court held that this act was in violation of the **Juvenile Justice Act**, that only a child welfare board could determine how the girls were to be released. The Court then set forth guidelines for courts dealing with girls taken from brothels in the future. This case is significant because victims of trafficking may need counseling and other medical services in order to prevent their re-victimization.

Balwant Singh v. State of Punjab Supreme Court of India (1987)

Sexual Violence and Rape

A woman was kidnapped and raped by men who owed her father money. The police decided to drop the case because they believed the charge was invented to harm the father's debtors. The Court held that the father's relationship with the defendants was insufficient to invalidate the victim's testimony.

Rajeev v. Ram Kishan Jaiswal Supreme Court of India (1992)

Dowry-related Violence, Harmful Traditional Practices

In this case, a woman's in-laws repeatedly demanded additional gifts from her. As a result of this harassment, the woman committed suicide. The Court defined dowry as any demand for gifts in relation to marriage and dowry death as a death within seven years of marriage where there have been demands for dowry.

CEHAT v. Union of India Supreme Court of India (2001)

Female Infanticide and Foeticide, Femicide, Harmful Traditional Practices

In this public interest litigation, an NGO that works on health issues challenged the government's failure to adequately address the issue of anti-girl child sex selection and the enforcement of the laws prohibiting prenatal sex identification. The Court ordered the government to respond with what it planned to do to address the problem.

Sakshi v. Union of Inda Supreme Court Supreme Court of India (2004)

Sexual Violence and Rape

In this public interest litigation, the Supreme Court ordered the use of extensive measures to protect children during sexual abuse trials.

Delhi Domestic Working Women's Forum v. Union of India Supreme Court of India (1991)

Gender-based Violence in General, Sexual Violence and Rape

In this public interest litigation, the case at issue concerned six women who were sexually assaulted and raped on a commuter train. The Court set out new requirements for police dealing with rape victims, including that victims be provided with legal representation, informing the victim of all her rights before questioning her, and protecting her anonymity during trial. The court also ordered that the **Criminal Compensation Board** consider the totality of the circumstances, ranging from the emotional pain of the act itself to medical costs and emotional pain associated with any child that might result from the rape when setting out compensation to be paid.

Dr. G.M. Natarajan v. State, Supreme Court Supreme Court of India (1995)

Gender-based Violence in General, Harmful Traditional Practices

A woman, harassed by her husband and in-laws for additional dowry, committed suicide by jumping into a well with her baby. The trial court acquitted the accused because the prosecution did not prove the case. The Court reversed, holding that if the facts necessary to create a presumption of dowry-death are shown, the burden of proof shifts to the defendant and not the prosecution.

Madan Gopal Kakkad v. Naval Dubey Supreme Court of India (1992)

Statutory Rape or Defilement

A man attempted to have vaginal sex with an eight-year-old girl, but did not break her hymen. The Court held that even the slightest penetration meets the definition for rape.

Air India v. Nargesh Meerza Supreme Court of India (1981)

Abortion and Reproductive Health Rights, Gender Discrimination

Air India, a state-owned company, required female flight attendants to retire under three circumstances: (1) upon reaching 35 years of age, (2) upon getting married, or (3) upon first pregnancy. The Court struck the rules down, holding that these requirements constituted official arbitrariness and hostile discrimination.

Association for Social Justice Research v. Union of India Supreme Court of India (2010)

Harmful Traditional Practices

A father married his 11/12 year old daughter to an adult man. When an NGO intervened, the father and "husband" argued that no money had been exchanged and that the girl would have a better life in marriage. The Court held that marriage of a minor girl is presumptively invalid unless the girl decides otherwise when she reaches 18 years of age.

Bachcha v. State of U.P. Supreme Court of India (2007)

Sexual Violence and Rape, StatutoryRape or Defilement

A man took a six-year-old girl into his house, removed her clothes and masturbated until he ejaculated on her stomach. The prosecution charged that he was found in the act of raping the girl, but the medical evidence showed that he could not have done so. The Court held that he could be found guilty of an "offence to modesty," which the court defined as any action that would be shocking the sense of decency of a woman. Here, the Court finds the perpetrator guilty despite India's inadequate criminal law to deal with sexual assault not amounting to rape.

National Commission for Women

The National Commission for Women (NCW) is a statutory body established in January 1992 under the 1990 **National Commission for Women's Act**. It's mandate is to advise the government on all policy matters concerning women, to review legislations and to intervene or initiate proceedings in the Supreme Court on matters concerning women.

Functions of the Commission

1) The commission shall perform all or any of the following functions, namely :-

a. investigate and examine all matters relating to the safeguards provided for women under the Constitution and other laws;

b. present to the Central Government, annually and at such other times as the Commission may deem fit, reports upon the working of those safeguard;

c. make in such reports/recommendations for the effective implementation of those safeguards for improving the conditions of women by the Union or any state;

d. review, from time to time, the exiting provisions of the Constitution and other laws affecting women and recommend amendments thereto so as to suggest remedial legislative measures to meet any lacunae, inadequacies or shortcomings in such legislations;

e. take up cases of violation of the provisions of the Constitution and of other laws relating to women with the appropriate authorities;

f. look into complaints and take suo moto notice of matters relating to:-
i. deprivation of women's rights;

ii. non-implementation of laws enacted to provide protection to women and also to achieve the objective of equality and development; iii. non-compliance of policy decisions, guidelines or instructions aimed at mitigating hardships and ensuring welfare and providing relief to women, and take up the issues arising out of such matters with appropriate authorities;

g) call for special studies or investigations into specific problems or situations arising out of discrimination and atrocities against women and identify the constraints so as to recommend strategies for their removal;

h) undertake promotional and educational research so as to suggest ways of ensuring due representation of women in all spheres and identify factors responsible for impeding their advancement, such as, lack of access to housing and basic services, inadequate support services and technologies for reducing drudgery and occupational health hazards and for increasing their productivity;

i) participate and advice on the planning process of socio-economic development of women;

j) evaluate the progress of the development of women under the Union and any State;

k) inspect or cause to inspect a jail, remand home, women's institution or other place of custody where women are kept as prisoners or otherwise and take up with the concerned authorities for remedial action, if found necessary;

l) fund litigation involving issues affecting a large body of women;

m) make periodical reports to the Government on any matter pertaining to women and in particular various difficulties under which women toil;

n) Any other matter which may be referred to it by Central Government.

2) The Central Government shall cause all the reports referred to in clause (b) of sub-section

a) to be laid before each House of Parliament along with memorandum explaining the action taken or proposed to be taken on the recommendations relating to the Union and the reasons for the non-acceptance, if any, of any such recommendations.

Powers of the Commission

While conducting investigations, the Commission has the powers of a civil court to summon any person, examine the person on oath, discovery and production of document, to receive evidence on affidavits, requisition, public record and issue commissions for examination of witnesses and documents

Working of the Commission

The Commission processes the complaints received verbally or in writing. It also takes into account suo moto (on its own) notice of cases related to women. The complaints received relate to various categories of crimes against women such as domestic violence, harassment, dowry, torture, murder, kidnapping/abduction, complaints against NRI marriages, desertion, bigamy, rape, police harassment, brutality, cruelty by husband, deprivation of rights, gender discrimination, sexual harassment at workplace and so on. The complaints are acted upon in the following manner:

Specific cases of police apathy are sent to the police authorities for

- investigation and cases are monitored. Family disputes are resolved or compromises struck through counselling.

- disaggregated data are made available to various state authorities to facilitate action. In sexual harassment complaints, the concerned organizations are urged to

- expedite cases and the disposal is monitored. For serious crimes, the Commission constitutes an Inquiry Committee to

- provide immediate relief and justice to the victims of violence and atrocities.

Strategies of the Commission

In keeping with its mandate, the Commission evolved the following strategies to improve upon the status of women and women development:

- economic empowerment through building-up skills and securing access to gainful employment. Political empowerment through awareness, training and mobilization for

- equitable representation in all fora. Prevention of violence and discrimination against women inside and outside

- the home through legal reform and sensitive enforcement.

Amelioration of conditions of disadvantaged women, such as:

a) Physically challenged women including those who are visually disabled or mentally affected.

b) Socially challenged women including Muslim women, women from Scheduled Caste and Scheduled Tribes, widows and prostitutes.

c) Prevention of indecent representation of women in the media through legal and social sanctions. Achievements **Prepared Gender Profiles of all states and UTs except Lakshadweep. Please check**

- Took up women related issues and was proactive in Parivarik Mahila Lok

- Adalats. Reviewed laws such as Dowry Prohibition Act, 1961, PNDT Act 1994,

- Indian Penal Code 1860 and the National Commission for Women Act, 1990 to make them more stringent and effective. Organized workshops/ consultations, etc.

Parivarik Mahila Lok Adalats

The National Commission of Women has evolved an innovative concept of Parivarik Mahila Lok Adalat (PMLA), which supplements the efforts of the District Legal Service Authority (DLSA) for redressal and speedy disposal of the matters related to marriage and family affairs pending in various courts. The Parivarik Mahila Lok Adalat functions on the model of the Lok Adalat. The Commission provides financial assistance to NGOs or State Women Commissions or State Legal Service Authority to organize the Parivarik Mahila Lok Adalat. The objectives of Parivarik Mahila Lok Adalat are as follows:

- To provide speedy and cost-free dispensation of justice to women

- To generate awareness among the public regarding conciliatory mode of dispute settlement.

- To gear up the process of organizing the Lok Adalats and to encourage the public

- To settle their disputes outside the formal set-up. To empower public especially women to participate in justice delivery mechanism.

Issues around working of NCW

The major issues around working of the National Commission for Women are as follows:

NCW's functions are dependent on the grants offered by the central government. Financial assistance provided to the Commission is inadequate to meet its needs. NCW's members are appointed by the government and the commission does not have power to select its own members. NCW lacks concrete legislative power. It enjoys power only to recommend amendments and submit reports. The recommendations of the NCW are not binding on the Union or state governments. Often it takes action only if the issues are brought to light. Unreported cases of suppression and oppression are generally ignored by the Commission. NCW's jurisdiction is not operative in Jammu and Kashmir.

Drawbacks

It has no actual legislative powers. It only has the powers to suggest amendments and submit reports which are not obligatory on state or Union Governments. It does not have the power to choose its own members. The power selecting members is vested with the Union Government and the nature of country's volatile political scenario tends the commission to be politicized. It is reliant on financial assistance from the Union Government and this couldcompromise the independence of the Commission.

About Majlis

Our Motto: Transforming Victims into Survivors—Transforming a victim into a survivor is a long drawn process. It is not a matter of merely changing the vocabulary, while keeping intact an oppressive system which constantly re-victimizes her, causes her extreme trauma and brings her down several notches in the social ladder from where she was, prior to the abuse. She becomes a survivor only when she emerges stronger for having walked through this intimidating system, with someone extending a helping hand, and in the process transforms the system itself, rendering it more humane. It is our hope that having responded to their needs, we helped each of them to overcome their vulnerabilities, and attain their goals and aspirations, beyond their 'case' and become survivors. Our programs litigation & socio-legal support helps survivors of sexual and domestic violence access justice and avail of services they are entitled to. We ensure that the dignity of the victim is maintained at all times.

Policy Interventions and Public Campaigns to place women's rights on the public policy agenda. Training and Awareness to State and Community

- Implementation of Laws Training Judiciary, Police, Medical Officers, Protection Officer and Public Administration.

- 'Know your Rights' for organizations, colleges, schools and community

- Para Legal Understanding for Social Workers (PLUS)

- Protection from Sexual Harassment at Workplace: a program to help organizations implement the policy and help the Internal Committee.

Sources

1. Bare acts

2. Ipleader.com

THE END